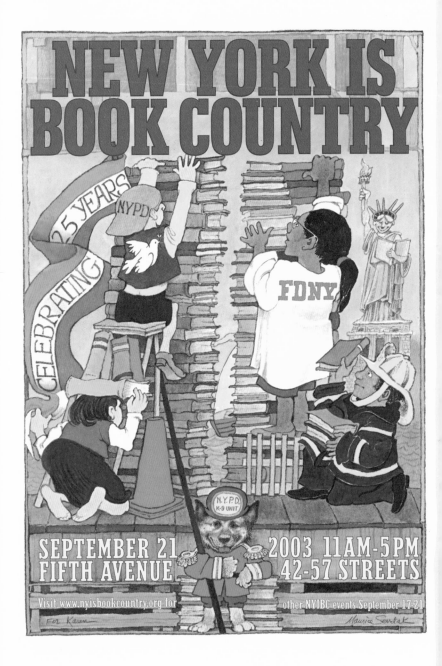

METROPOLIS FOUND

. . . .

METROPOLIS FOUND

NEW YORK IS BOOK COUNTRY
25TH ANNIVERSARY
COLLECTION

Proceeds from book sales will benefit New York Is Book
Country in its ongoing efforts to promote the joys of reading
and writing and to provide ongoing financial support to
the New York Public Libraries.

· ·

The Board of Directors of New York Is Book Country dedicates

Metropolis Found to Linda C. Exman,

the organization's founder who served as its

first Chairman of the Board and subsequently as

President through 2002.

Linda's vision and persistence were the driving force behind

the success of New York Is Book Country since its inception

twenty-five years ago. Her integrity and spirit, along with her

desire to provide the readers and writers of New York City

with a cherished event, will never be forgotten.

Thank you, Linda, for twenty-five years of

New York Is Book Country.

CONTENTS

ACKNOWLEDGMENTS

New York Is Book Country is grateful to so many people who lent their time and talent to *Metropolis Found.*

First and foremost, we wish to acknowledge the gracious participation of our wonderful authors, whose beautiful work is between these pages.

Thank you to contributing editor Linda C. Exman, whose spirited cajoling and tireless follow-through gained the participation of our talented authors.

We also thank Jenny Frost, publisher extraordinaire, and Doug Pepper, a brilliant editor, as well as their extended family at Crown Publishers, who produced and published this book. These wonderfully creative and enthusiastic people include: Amy Boorstein, Whitney Cookman, Nina Frieman, Juleyka Lantigua,

Lindsay Mergens, Marysarah Quinn, Tim Roethgen, Mari Sheedy, Thaline Tarpinian, and the many others who contributed their talent and energy.

To the printers and suppliers who donated their time, their products, and their services to this book, we thank you as well. They include: Coral Graphics Services, Digital Composition Services, Domtar Inc., Dynamic Graphic Finishing, Ecological Fibers, Inc., RR Donnelley, and Tri-Plex Packaging.

Many thanks to Jim Chandler, Audrey Seitz, Susan Abel, and all of the folks at the Ingram Book Company for actively and freely distributing and selling this book.

A special thank you to Roger Bilheimer and Sally Dedecker for their advice and guidance.

And, finally, a heartfelt thanks to everyone on the board of New York Is Book Country for their support and enthusiasm, without which we could not have succeeded.

COURTNEY MULLER
Executive Director
New York Is Book Country

. . . .

METROPOLIS FOUND

INTRODUCTION
LINDA C. EXMAN

F ROM THE MOMENT the last booth was disassembled after the first New York Is Book Country street fair in September 1979, we could hardly wait for our press notices. Imagine our delight when we finally opened *The New York Times* to read, "The book fair that occupied Fifth Avenue's sidewalks last Sunday between Forty-seventh and Fifty-seventh Streets attracted so many people that fears of widespread illiteracy seemed for the day unjustified."

We knew we were on to something.

Editorial writers from the other dailies also signaled their approval. The *New York Post* described the occasion as, "a splendid affair, a joyous celebration," and observed that, "despite a couple of promising football games and several other neighborhood fairs, many thousands preferred to spend the afternoon browsing among the books."

The *Daily News* agreed: "The event celebrated the Big Apple's place as the book publishing capital of the nation . . . in such an upbeat, stylish way that we would like to see the book fair become an annual event," and called the gathering of some 200,000 fairgoers "one of the best behaved crowds of that size in the city's history."

Now, twenty-five years later, the one-day street fair is a cherished annual tradition, the core of a five-day, citywide festival, with an ever-expanding schedule during the year that includes programs in the schools, writing workshops, and other book-oriented events. The players may change over the decades, but the annual effort continues uninterrupted, thanks to NYIBC's small but hardworking staff, its dedicated board of directors, and its legions of volunteers, both in and out of the book industry. We're proud that Book Country's example has served as the prototype for book fairs in Miami, San Francisco, Seattle, Nashville, Washington, D.C., and other cities across the country.

What better way to celebrate this milestone year

than by publishing a Silver Anniversary sampler of original pieces by some of our favorite local writers? The authors represented here have all played significant roles in Book Country's success—speaking at various events, serving on the Advisory Council and other committees, visiting the schools, judging NYIBC's student Reading Bees, recording public service radio announcements, gracing our fund raisers as guests of honor, drawing thousands of their fans to the Sunday street fair, and helping in countless other ways. I have been singularly privileged to be associated with such generous and talented people in this enterprise for more than two dozen years.

Each of the offerings you're about to read has been written expressly for this collection. With New York on their minds, the contributors offer an entertaining and thoughtful mix of personal recollections, stories, and poems, all filled with the wit, energy, and style this town is known for. Their thoughts range widely, often extending way beyond the city's urban confines, and the particular becomes universal as the reader shares the experiences of these gifted writers.

United States Poet Laureate Billy Collins sets the stage with an evocative ode to the city and its millions of book lovers. From there, topics go on to cover a broad spectrum, from lighthearted advice for entertaining out-of-town visitors to the deeply considered answer to a young Silicon Valley mogul's question, "Actually, can you give me one good reason why I should read a book again?"

A variety of takes on the immigrant experience—Cuban, Haitian, and Puerto Rican, and by those hailing from the Midwest, Deep South, and APO addresses around the world—exist side-by-side with native New Yorkers' charming, but unsentimental accounts of growing up in "The Neighborhood." You'll be able to smell the chalk and erasers between the lines of a poet's pure memory of her first day at school, and taste an incipient food writer's astonished initial adventures with ethnic cuisine.

Humorously or poignantly, always movingly, two authors chronicle the way their lifelong love affairs with books were launched by a beloved parent. Others give us rare glimpses of the creative imagination at work. We learn how a chance encounter with a fellow Vietnam veteran lit the slow fuse that ignited a best-selling novelist's career. And how an unstoppable passion "to tell our stories" to children sparked the establishment of an award-winning African-American publishing company. A prolific fiction writer with a huge global audience owns up comically to the perverse pleasures he finds in that necessary evil: translation!

Some authors make references to their experiences at NYIBC's famous street fair. In a short fiction piece, a mystery writer takes a different tack, imagining one of her most popular recurring character's finding unexpected inspiration—in the form of the perfect book title—while strolling the fair. A true story chronicles a working class kid's ascent from "the bottom rung on the publishing ladder" (unpacking cartons in a book warehouse) to the pinch-me-it's-not-real success who knows he's arrived when confronted with a three-booth display of his works on Fifth Avenue.

Moments of magic are found in these pages—in a true, time-travel story from a writer of children's books, and in a novelist's invention of an unlikely superhero. A mystery writer departs from her usual genre to portray the crushing loneliness of an accomplished Somebody, forced to confront life without her closest friend. In edgy, unexpected ways, a poet conveys the assured contrariness of the City, recognizable to anyone who has ever set foot on its potholed asphalt.

A book of this kind, written at this moment in history, will inevitably include references to present-day realities. Since the bewildering horror and lingering shock of the events of September 11, 2001, are never far from the minds of many of us, it's not surprising that reflections on that era-ending day inform more than one of the eloquent essays gathered here.

After our book fair had to be canceled in the wake of those events, it was unclear whether exhibitors would return in 2002 in the usual numbers, or if, indeed, fairgoers would be present in the customary tens of thousands. Happily, when the day dawned last year, the book community turned out in force. There were even more booths from publishers and booksellers than had been scheduled for the previous year, and readers and writers crowded the streets in gratifying tribute to the enduring appeal of that miraculous package called, "the book."

Maya Angelou writes, "I am a book person and I sense myself correct when I feel the heft of a book in my hand or on my lap." For all those who feel the same way—New Yorkers born, bred, resident, or wannabe, and for anyone who has ever savored the work of a New York writer—this book is for you.

New York City

Linda C. Exman is the founder of New York Is Book Country. She served as its first Chairman of the Board and subsequently as President through 2002.

KEYNOTE POEM

THE CITY
BILLY COLLINS

At dusk, a woman with a view of the river
turns away from the window
and passes through a doorway
into the vaulted room of *Middlemarch.*

The man who faces a brick wall
pulls down the shade
and enters the long hallway
of *The Poems of Delmore Schwartz.*

So many windows in the city,
facing other windows
across the streaming avenues
or the tiny garden with its broken pot.

So many eyes and stacks of books,
and there is no stopping the clouds
drifting over the spires and the bridges,
the sun weakening over the Hudson,

nor the loud report from the streets
and the sudden lift of pigeons—
and what we see if we peer now
like angels into these evening windows:

the woman absorbed in a chair,
the man prone in a citrine circle of light.

BOOK COUNTRY

MAYA ANGELOU

A H, THE SPLENDOR of a festival. The very mention of it brings memories of sunlight and laughter, of music, food, good friends, and affable strangers. When the thought of books is added to the remembered delights of a festival, I am transported to an experience I had at New York City Is Book Country years ago.

Certain streets in Gotham were closed and book lovers roamed in and out of stalls furnished with tomes, offered by mysterious mystery writers, fey children's book authors, scientific academic professors, knowledgeable biographers, poor, but elegant poets, and elite novelists whose books were destined to sell in the millions.

The atmosphere was delicious. People acted as if they attended book festivals every weekend of their lives. Children darted in and around their families' legs. Some dogs attended, bringing their owners on short leashes.

People flirted with everyone or pontificated to anyone, on any subject, which came to their minds. Shills enticed onlookers to step into the tent, "Look at this book. Isn't it a beauty?"

I stayed in the wondrous tumble until my calves and feet insisted that I was torturing them. When I took them to the nearest bar to be restored, I realized I had had a great time rubbing shoulders with book people. I was better for having been there, and I imagined all the other attendees shared my feelings.

I am a book person and I sense myself correct when I feel the heft of a book in my hand or on my lap.

I have always found the description "Private Library" to be a contradiction in terms. School, city, and county libraries, even three or four books, held in place by bookends, contain ideas thought by people all over the world. Those who have shared their ideas down the centuries since they scratched them on scrolls of papyrus are represented here.

Although I am too responsible to steal a book, I confess I do feel very free around books.

It is my great joy to visit a library, any library. When I stand before the Majesty of the New York City Library I carry myself as if I am utterly erudite. When I climb those gracious stairs, I could be walking to paradise, or just going to have my library card updated.

ALL CHANGED,
CHANGED UTTERLY

LAWRENCE BLOCK

I WAS TEN AND A HALF when I fell in love with New York. That was in December of 1948, when my father and I took the train down from Buffalo to spend a long weekend in the city of his birth. We rode the subways and the Third Avenue El, saw Ray Bolger in *Where's Charley?*, went to Bedloe's Island to gape at the Statue of Liberty, and caught a live telecast of *Toast of the Town*, which is what Ed Sullivan was then calling his Sunday night program. (I'd never seen television until then; I was more impressed by the monitors than by what was happening onstage.) We stayed at the Hotel Commodore next to Grand Central, so I suppose we must have slept, but I don't remember that part.

As soon as I could manage it, I moved to New York, and right away I began setting my fiction here. Still do. Most of my books take place in New York. Bernie Rhodenbarr and Matt Scudder rarely leave the five boroughs, while Keller and Tanner, who venture far afield, always come home to Manhattan. When my wife and I moved to Florida in the mid-eighties, I still set everything in New York. What else could I do? What the hell did I know about Florida?

People have said that the city is a virtual character in my fiction, a presence that informs the work far beyond street names and subway lines. Any number of them, New Yorkers and others, were outraged when Hollywood transplanted Matt Scudder to Los Angeles (*Eight Million Ways to Die*) and Bernie Rhodenbarr to San Francisco (*Burglar*). I know that New York energizes my work, and that I'd be no more inclined to situate my work elsewhere than I would to (God forbid) live somewhere else.

A decade or so ago, I realized I ought to write a big New York novel, a book that was somehow not merely of the city but about the city, a massive robust multiple-viewpoint book with all the New York I could cram into it. Someday, I told myself, and went on to Other Things.

Then a little later, in 1993, I came across a quotation from John Gunther, a rich paean to the city, saying how big and bustling and wonderful the place is, and ending with the line: ". . . but it becomes a small town when it rains."

Beautiful, I thought, and all at once I had a title for the book I seemed unlikely ever to write. *A Small Town When It Rains?* Not quite. *A Small Town in the Rain?* Still a little awkward, but it was there somewhere . . .

Come December of 2000 I realized it was time. My publishers at Morrow/HarperCollins were ecstatic at the prospect of a big multiple-viewpoint nonseries thriller, and the title had refined itself to *Small Town.* Now all I had to do was figure out something for it to be about, and then sit down and write it.

In the summer of 2001 I went to work, and by the end of August I had a little more than a hundred pages done and four or five principal characters introduced and in motion. I took a couple of weeks off, and then 9/11 happened. Way down on the long list of casualties was *Small Town*. Not that I felt like writing anyway, not that I cared much what I wrote next, or if I wrote anything . . . but the book, it seemed to me, was dead in the water. It was set in a pre–9/11 city, a city that had ceased to exist.

As I said, it didn't matter much. Nine months went by during which time I didn't even attempt to write anything. I don't remember what I did, actually. This and that, I suppose. I write a lot, but I don't write all the time, and it's very much in my nature to take time off. This was more time off than usual, but not unprecedented; I had time booked in a writers' colony in June and July of 2002 and assumed I'd write something then.

I had no idea what it might be. It seemed to me that a New York novel of any sort was impossible. It would either be about 9/11, which was a horrible idea, or it would NOT be about 9/11, which was arguably worse. I thought some piece of fluff—a Bernie Rhodenbarr book, say—might work, but was that what I wanted to do? One thing was sure. I wouldn't be working on *Small Town*.

I surprised myself, though. Because three weeks before my colony stay I printed out *Small Town*, and a week before I drove out there I actually read what I'd printed out, and I liked what I'd read. It had to be recast, certainly, and the time frame was wrong; it had to take place not before but after the terrorist attacks. And it had to be a different story, a much bigger story.

Writing is magic, and I say this not boastfully but in wonder. I'm not the magician, waving his wand, pulling a rabbit out of a hat. I'm not sure what I am. The wand, maybe. Or the rabbit, or even the hat. Who cares? It's all magic.

And, magically, I sat down at my desk the day I got to the colony, and five weeks later *Small Town* was written. It didn't feel as though I were channeling the book, or taking down celestial dictation. It felt like work, but work I couldn't keep from doing. Some years back the Red Sox had a spirited left-hander of whom it was said that he pitched like a man with his hair on fire. Well, I wrote like a man with his hair on fire, and what came out was *Small Town*. It wound up much longer and darker and richer than the book I'd had originally in mind, with a very different story line. My agent read it and did back flips. My publishers, here and abroad, were over the moon. As I write these lines, the book's publication is a week away, and the only really important verdict—the readers'—is yet to come. By the time you read this, it'll be in.

But whether or not *Small Town* turns out to be what New Yorkers want to read, it is very definitely the book this New Yorker needed to write. It is, I came to realize, a post-apocalyptic novel set in New York in the summer of 2002. We've had our apocalypse, and we're New Yorkers, and we're moving on.

6 DECEMBER 2002
TONYA BOLDEN

I.

he has my nine-ninety-nine per pound parmesan in hand
grate it?
no, i smile
he smiles back, weighs the wedge

i've got seven-forty-nine worth and he,
still a smile as he slaps the price onto plastic wrap
grazie, bella
grazie, i nod, i smile

an elderly italian who
slices cold cuts

weighs cheese

scoops up salads: quarter-pound, half-pound, whatever-

    the-customer-wants—

this man

without leer to the lip

without a tease of sleaze in his eyes

has

made

my

day

bella

do i look the part?

nose still cold from the cold

eyes still in sorta-shock from so much white trudged

    through, by

to reach this bronx met food

bundled in a five- six- nine-year-old soldier-green

parka-type coat, head

swaddled in autumnal-patterned shawl-scarf

capped by cheap black knitty

spirit chapped

. . . .

grungy red gloves inside the wnyc canvas tote i
tote to the market
so as not to take up so many plastic bags
so as not to contribute
　　　(so much)
to the trashing of america
bella

when you are over forty and have lost your mother and
　　finally understand why
when you were young
women older than your mother *always* had hand lotion
　　in their handbags—

when you come to see gray hair has a will of her own—

when *that's youth for you!* is common in your parlance—

when you wonder how you might contend with days of
　　depends and
attend to ads for undereye creams—

you are not nonchalant about a *grazie, bella*

i'm flashbacked to wonder years in a part of harlem
    where eye-talians
part of the norm alongside ricans and
my people morphing from negro to black
bella

and i loved that carnival in july
herald of the festival starring a gigantor lady saint i
    never prayed to
    (not being catholic)
being carried round-around the block
and people cheered
and i ate five-cent fruit ices
bella

so nice
needed on the day i learned from aol
al qaeda might have holiday gifts for us

again? i wonder
as i've wondered other autumn, winter, spring,
    summer, wintry autumn days
my hometown?
my still-bruised new york?
again?

shopping for food, provisioning up
calms my nerves

II.

sad but soothing on the way home
lapsing into memories of my city before
long before
the ugly day

back when the empire
the tallest
some subway seats still like wicker
tokens tiny like dimes

back when there was no cable
back when there was woolworths
back when there were no play dates   instead
doorbell belled   or
intercom buzzed—
can tonya come out-n-play?

back when yorkville
closer to quaint, dotted with descendants of old world
     shops, where

mommy picked out special spices

delicacies for holiday meals   or

seven-layer cake   or

maybe marzipan

for my birthday   or

just because

i

was

her

child

back when an egg cream

not so uncommon

breakfast at dubrows a saturday morning extra when i

    went to work with daddy,

to the rag trade:

him working

me working

       (stamp-stamp-stamping o'grady & bialer on

          bills of lading, envelopes, boxes)

me taking my work serious

       (daddy said it was important!)

me trying to stamp *real-real* straight

me hanging around by his side

me over the years

naturally

organically

learning

chanukah gilt, gefilte fish, whitefish, lox, sittin shiva

and having fond memories of redhead belle sending
    the family

a few pounds of her ownmade chopped liver in
    decembers

back when living multicultural

was not a work, an agenda, just

the everyday way of a life

baychester had more bluejays

and some summer evenings the sharpening man

        (scissors, knives, lawn mower blades)

cruised the block hoping for business

and eggs and milk a milkman delivered, really dressed
    in white

and mommy

dinnered us with chicken, turkey, ground round, pig
    knuckles, sausage, mutton, from

gruff-but-nice-smiling

twinkle-eyed

accent-light-italian phil

who never called my mother *bella* i don't think:

hello, mrs. bolden, what can i get ya today, mrs. bolden?

  i can orderem for ya, mrs. bolden

cornish hens i so loved, a sometimes or once-a-year treat, like

dinner in chinatown

sightseeing christmas lights in westchester

sightseeing the groovy in the village—

daddy, can we go to the bowery?

daddy sometimes obliging

not asking why baby girl likes to sightsee people it used to be okay to call

bums, but

daddy

  (and mommy)

pearling the grim adventure into a lesson:

on counting your blessings

on praying for the less fortunate

on what not to be when you grow up

back when white castle car hops quick-snapped yellow
    trays onto windows of cars

        (most without ac)

wore minis

even when the hawk was out

and nyc had drive-ins and a child could delight in a
    drive out to the nearest

mcdonalds

        (in jersey)

        (not much more to the menu than hamburger,
            cheeseburger, shakes, fries)

        (nothing super-sized)

or to the paramus dairy queen, where

one july day we crowded around our long silver-gray
    oldsmobile, her radio loud

cheering one man's one small step

and i reach home with provisions

a bit stronger, braver

braced for this twenty-first-century life.

GIRL'S GUIDE TO NEW YORK THROUGH THE MOVIES

MEG CABOT

ALTHOUGH I'VE ALWAYS loved to read, my reading matter of choice prior to the age of twenty-two consisted almost exclusively of historical romance novels and *Star Wars* comic books.

So it is probably not surprising that, before moving to New York City—straight out of college, and from the heart of the Midwest—the only thing I knew about the Big Apple was what I had garnered from the movies.

And though I was in for a bit of a rough ride at first—I hadn't seen any movies depicting New York City garbage and phone service strikes, both of which were underway when I arrived in Manhattan in 1989—movie lore continues to serve as my guide to the big city, and has yet to fail me. Consider:

GHOST—This movie convinced me that it is easy for sculptors to find affordable and enormous lofts in Soho. Although I have since become disabused of this notion, lingering doubt remains: maybe if I had just looked long enough, I, too, could have found a 2,800-square-foot duplex with parquet floors for $900 a month and no broker's fee.

ROSEMARY'S BABY—The Dakota really is just as dark and spooky inside as it is in the movie. But you still can't beat it for an unimpeded view of the Macy's Thanksgiving Day Parade.

DAYLIGHT—This thriller starring Sylvester Stallone, who becomes trapped inside a flooded Holland Tunnel after an explosion, has caused me to scrutinize closely every door marked Personnel Only along the tunnel as I whiz past them. I've also memorized the locations of all the fire extinguishers down there, in case I need to grab one and use it to knock down the Personnel Only door in order to escape the roaring waters of the Hudson River.

BREAKFAST AT TIFFANY'S—I fell for this movie's erroneous assertion that living in a walk-up can be charming, when in truth, there is nothing charming about it at all: you have to take out your own trash, and there is no doorman to ward off the UPS guy while you are busy working on your novel. No wonder George Peppard's character never got any work done while he was living in one!

FUNNY FACE—Another misleader: the dark Greenwich Village bookshop in which Audrey Hepburn is discovered by photographer Fred Astaire looks very sweet and inviting. But as any girl who frequents dark bookshops in Manhattan knows, they are just breeding grounds for bearded men in sandals with socks who try to hit on you by asking what you think of David Eggers's new book. *Ew!* (To the guys in the socks, not Dave Eggers.)

THE TAKING OF PELHAM ONE TWO THREE— I have ridden the subway for almost fifteen years now, and never once has my train been hijacked by Robert Shaw. But hope springs eternal.

SPIDER-MAN—I always thought that the Roosevelt Island cable car looked dangerous, and now that I know how easily the Green Goblin can sever it from its moorings, I for one will find alternate transportation in the unlikely event that I am ever invited to Roosevelt Island for brunch or something.

QUICKSILVER—There is some dispute over in which city, exactly, this movie is set. But there is no disputing that in it, Kevin Bacon plays a failed stock trader who becomes a bicycle messenger. The film's denouement seems to take place in the meat packing district, where Kevin races—on a bike—the evil Gypsy, who is driving a car. Not to give away the ending, but if you know of an overpass downtown that ends in a sudden drop off into the Hudson, could you please contact me?

MOONSTRUCK—I have no interest whatsoever in opera, but the scene where Cher is at the Met with Nicolas Cage, and the lights start going up—up! By themselves!—entranced me as a teen. I had to see this phenomenon for myself, and so scored tickets to *Medea* early in my first year in Manhattan. The lights were as big a thrill in person as they were on film. *Medea* I could have done without, but whatever.

*SPECIAL NOTE: *Moonstruck* is also a movie at the conclusion of which I heard a fellow Hoosier—seated not far from me at the Von Lee Theater in Bloomington, Indiana—breathe as the lights came up, "Oh, I just love movies about Jewish people!"

WHEN HARRY MET SALLY—It's not the Katz's deli scene, which is great but could have happened in my hometown, that always got to me. Instead, it's the scene where Harry gets out of the station wagon in front of the arch at Washington Square. If you look through the arch behind Billy Crystal, you can see the Twin Towers. The towers quickly came to serve as my compass for finding the direction of downtown. The fact that you can no longer see the towers through the Washington Square arch is troubling, but witnessing their collapse did serve to cement forever my resolve never to live anywhere else.

Now that I have lived in New York for more than a decade, I have contributed my own fictional interpretation of it to the public consciousness, though in the movie version of my book, *The Princess Diaries*, my characters have been mysteriously transported to San Francisco. In Mia Thermopolis's Manhattan, however, the Twin Towers are still standing; my favorite Chinese restaurants—Great Shanghai and Number One Noodle Son—are still serving. But Mia's Cote d'Azur principality of Genovia will always pale in comparison to my kingdom of choice, the city that never sleeps.

E SPRE SSO

CHARLOTTE CARTER

*S*TILL IN HER PAJAMAS, she blew the dust
from the lid of the oval box and then sorted
through some 200 snapshots. But she was unable to
find a single photograph of Russell. That was weird.

On the other hand, maybe it did make sense. Now
that she thought about it, their friendship was kind of a
secret.

Not that they had anything to hide.

Mandy and Russell had seen dozens of movies
together, they had been meeting for drinks or dinner for years, gone to museums, stolen half days
from work to walk through the park eating chocolates
from a box, met for quick afternoon coffee, spent

long evenings in dives. But never in the company of any of their mutual friends. Always just the two of them.

Owen, her lover of many years, had left earlier that morning, before she awoke. Actually, she'd heard him lock the front door and then come back into the apartment for something he had forgotten. But she had not called out to him.

She went into the kitchen and poured into a small cup what was left of the coffee Owen had made for himself. It was tepid now. Some old words of his came back to her: "Only a woman would drink cold coffee." Out of context, it was a strange non sequitur. And indeed she had no memory of the context.

She had forgotten to take in the cleaning and laundry that week, and the two weeks prior. Probably that meant she'd be wearing something second tier to her lunch with Russell.

She meant to make the bed and then pick up the stray clothing, papers, and all that littered the room. But a few of the photos had slipped onto the floor, and within seconds after she bent to retrieve them, she was lost in patching through all the pictures again, one by one. Was she still looking for some image of Russell? Or were those faces from the past calling to her for their own reasons?

She caught sight of her dead brother as an infant. There was a shot of her the weekend in the 1980s she spent at her boss's summer home on the Vineyard. Several young women at a baby shower for a girl Mandy didn't see much of anymore. Her friend Frederic in full makeup and a flowy chiffon scarf in front of the Vertigo apartment house on Mason Street, in San Francisco.

Nostalgia is contemptible. Owen had said that too, deriding her keenness for silent movies.

This is stupid, Mandy thought, and shoved the dusty box under the bed.

11:45 now. It was going to be tight, but if she focused there'd be just enough time to bathe and give herself a facial, then dress and get to the restaurant a few minutes before one. Fortunately the place they'd chosen was no more than five minutes away on foot. In the tub, she savored the image of herself already seated at the table when he arrived, arms held out to him in greeting.

She was known at the nouvelle Italian restaurant. They gave her a corner banquette. The San Pellegrino was poured before she even finished removing her scarf.

The hippest of the new trattorias were all hiring willowy, dreadlocked black youngsters for the reception desk. Invariably they were dark-skinned youngsters, closer to Russell's color than to hers. Mandy had a quick aural memory then: she heard herself asking her grandmother why the children playing in the street on which her family owned property called her yellow. "They're ignorant," Gran said. "We are not yellow, we're red."

Wasn't it amusing, how the Italian immigrants these days were competing with the French in their Negrophilia. A far cry from Little Italy in the old days. Well, there was no more Little Italy, was there? The Chinese had vanquished it. From Mulberry Street on the east and Canal from the north, their old racist community had been squeezed to a thin strip hardly deserving of the word neighborhood. Rough justice.

Russell, ten minutes late, was wearing a collarless pale green linen shirt she had never seen before. His hair was newly cut. It made him look like the young Louis Armstrong.

"I think I'll rip that right off your body," she said,

giving him a strong hug and two kisses on the mouth. He sat down, her hand still in his.

He was newly home from a stint at a small black college where as special lecturer he had taught identity theory for a semester.

He and Mandy had been introduced, all those years ago, by a mutual friend who was, like Russell, a rising black scholar. Mandy was just starting out in the world of nonprofit foundations. She was by now *Somebody* in New York—in Manhattan. But of course that was a very long list with hundreds of subsets.

"You look so healthy and rested, brother dear," she said.

"I feel good," Russell said. "You're looking beautiful, same as always."

"So tell. What was it like in the fair South? Magnolias in bloom? And who's the foreman down there again?"

Russell had no end of jokes about himself as a production line worker in the African-American studies factory.

"Sam Perry is the dean. He's pretty smart."

"You like him?"

"Yeah. He's nice."

Russell smiled crookedly, almost a grimace, and looked away from her.

Ah, she thought. He doesn't want to talk about this. Must've banged up against somebody's correctness. She signaled the waiter with her eyes. "Should I do the wine?" she asked.

"Bring it on," he said.

"You're not eating dessert? But you have to, honey. You know I like to watch."

He shrugged and relented.

"Either I'm crazy," she said, watching him scoop tiramisu from the tinted goblet, "or something's wrong."

His telling brown eyes misted over.

"I knew it," said Mandy. "What did they do to you? I'll kill them."

"I met someone," he said, almost in disbelief.

She picked up her lemon peel and drove it in circles around the lip of her cup. "Great."

"Amanda, I'm getting married."

He reached for her. She withdrew her hand, instinctively.

On the evening they first met, they were seated across from each other at a long table on the Upper West Side. The party went on long into the night. Mandy wasn't much of a drinker then and she was high on the perfect gimlets the stone-faced bartender kept handing her. Russell was the nicest man she had ever met, she decided, along with being one of the brightest. He was openhearted and funny and honest and not at all prissy about the Race. That night was a bona fide milestone, perhaps even a miracle. She had met someone and knew within minutes that they two would be great, loving friends. A miracle overdue. Mandy was not exactly pretty, but all sorts of people were drawn to her: other women, professors, shopkeepers, business contacts, street psychotics. She had almost stopped questioning the riddle of her choking loneliness. And so into her life came plain Russell in department store tweed, wildly intelligent, with skin smelling of blue family soap.

She was so intent on staking her claim to him, she barely noticed anyone else at the party, not even Owen Stein, an undisputed New York Somebody from the generation before hers, still commanding attention.

Literary movements came and went. Political figures. Eateries. Cultural obsessions. But Owen's post-War generation of Somebodies seemed to hold their ground.

At 2 A.M., Mandy and Russell were still deep in conversation, drunkenly picking over the last of the fresh pineapple at the abandoned dinner table. Red candlelight bathed her face as he asked, "Sleepy?" He ran his fingers along her forearm. "Are you freckled everywhere?"

"Oh, God, yes. I'm absolutely perforated with them. Aren't they grotesque? Guess what I'm making you when you come by for dinner. Soufflé."

"Is she young?" Mandy said.

"Yes."

Running through her mind now was the only thing she'd ever told Russell which he didn't understand. It was about scouring the ladies' shops on Delancey Street for a particular kind of minimizer bra. Mandy was due to have a business tea with a millionaire and it was her belief that large breasts intimidated old WASPs.

"How young?"

"She's Sam's daughter. The dean."

"A belle, Russell? You're marrying a Negro belle? Black cotillion shit?"

"Not that bad."

"Well, goodness, goodness. We'll just have to get her to trade in those ruffles for some basic New York black."

He shook his head.

"Oh, brother dear."

"Sam offered me a job."

"You're not, Russell . . . you're not . . . *Arkansas?*"

Back in the apartment, Mandy rooted around in Owen's desk until she found a cigarette. Still in her coat, she began to gather dirty towels and cotton undershirts, soiled sweaters and suit jackets. She sat down heavily on the Chinese bench, everything in her lap, feeling that nothing less than another miracle could give her the energy to rise again.

Eighteen years her senior, hidebound in his ways, and a Jew, Owen Stein had chosen her from among his female admirers in all age brackets. He had mentored, bullied, spoiled, waited for her, and loved her, enough to forgive in her the cowardice he despised in other people. He would be back in a few minutes from the panel he was moderating at the New School, and he would probably be hungry.

Slowly, she moved into the kitchen. It just seemed too great an effort to put together one of her famous sandwiches for him. She'd have to have something delivered. But, she thought, the very least she could do was to make a fresh pot of coffee.

ALVIRAH'S NEW YORK

MARY HIGGINS CLARK

"IT'S A BEAUTIFUL DAY for New York Is Book Country," Alvirah said happily, as she slid open the door and stepped out onto the terrace that overlooked Central Park. Beaming, she observed the picture-perfect September morning already being enjoyed in the park by early morning joggers and people of all ages on bicycles and skateboards. I bet the publishers will be thrilled. There will be a lot of people visiting their booths today, she thought.

"September is my favorite month," she sighed to her husband, Willy, who was hovering in the doorway, his hands outstretched to grab her in case the floor of the terrace gave way.

"Honey, every month is your favorite month. Please

come in. It makes me nervous to see you hanging over the edge like that."

"Willy, I've barely got my feet out of the living room," Alvirah protested, shaking her head. But she did step back into the living room. Willy's acrophobia was so severe that the one time he'd rushed onto the terrace because someone was trying to push her off it, he'd fainted dead away.

They were able to have this great apartment on Central Park South because four years ago they had won $40 million in the lottery. Before that Alvirah had been cleaning houses and Willy had been working as a plumber. Now in their mid-sixties, they were able to do exactly what they wanted. Alvirah had traded her vacuum cleaner and mop for a career as an amateur detective and contributing columnist to the *New York Globe*. Willy still kept the tools in his plumbing kit active but that was because he did so many repairs for the hard-up people being cared for by his formidable older sibling, Sister Cordelia.

They always went to the 10:15 Mass at St. Patrick's, then had brunch at the Peninsula Hotel. Today after the brunch they planned to stroll along Fifth Avenue and visit from booth to booth. Now that she was something of a celebrity because of the crimes she had solved, Alvirah knew many of the mystery writers who would be signing their books, and particularly wanted to chat with them. She had been approached by several publishers to write her own memoir starting with being raised in the Bronx, moving to Queens when she and Willy were married, and the interesting cases she had worked on.

The publisher she had signed up with did say to just give a tip-of-the hat to her life as a cleaning woman, but Alvirah objected strenuously to glossing over it. "You people think there's something wrong with helping folks to have nice, orderly lives," she'd pointed out. "I can't tell you how many marriages I saved by showing up once a week and keeping homes organized. There was one guy ready to either kill his wife or file for divorce because she was so untidy. I knew he really loved her and I told him to have me come in on Mondays and Fridays so nothing got too out of hand. It worked for the twenty years I was with them."

"I always was a good detective," she told her editor. "Another time I noticed that the husband was bringing some woman home when his wife was away on business. I nipped that one in the bud. I showed him the bar of soap his girlfriend had forgotten to take with her and said that I knew his wife was allergic to perfumed soap and that I'd left the vent on to make sure the scent didn't linger. He realized that he'd had a close call and thanked me. Then I told him that the reason his wife was still working and traveling was to save for a house because they wanted to start a family and that I thought some men would be smart enough to be grateful to have a partner like that. Let me tell you, I set him thinking. I didn't see any more signs of his lady friend, and two years later he and his wife bought a house. In New Rochelle. They have three lovely children now."

She was anxious to start the memoir but needed a title. She knew when she found it the book would flow like rain down the drain pipe.

All of that was running through Alvirah's mind as she made coffee, squeezed oranges, and toasted English muffins. Willy was already dressed, handsome as they come with his full head of white hair, twinkling blue eyes, and solid build. Everyone said he was the living image of Tip O'Neill, the legendary speaker of the House of Representatives.

She left Willy reading the *Times* while she show-ered, applied her makeup, fussed with her hair, and dressed in one of her new Escada pant suits. This one in a tweedy toast brown color went very well with her red hair newly restored to that shade by the colorist at Mr. Kenneth.

At quarter of ten, arm in arm, she and Willy began to walk down Fifth Avenue. The stalls were open and the early visitors were strolling along already filling their tote bags with books.

"This is the twenty-fifth anniversary of New York Is Book Country, and do you realize we haven't missed a one?" Alvirah said.

"One was rained out," Willy reminded her. "That was a deluge. I didn't dry out for a week."

"But we were here just in case a saint who loved to read interceded for us, and the sun came out. Willy, everyone thinks you change when you suddenly get rich. But I didn't need money to make me love to read. I had a book in my hand when other kids were still shaking their rattles. If God had blessed us with children, I'd have been reading to them while they were still in the womb."

"I know you would have, honey."

"I'll have that point in my memoir."

"I can't wait to read it," Willy said. "It'll be great."

"I know it will."

"Maybe I should have something about winning the lottery in the title," Alvirah said a moment later, now thinking aloud, a habit Willy understood.

"On the other hand I'd like to have New York in the title," she mused. "I mean, Willy, where else in the world is there a city like this?"

She answered her own question, "Nowhere."

They were passing The Mysterious Bookshop stall on Fifty-sixth Street when the answer came. The title. Like a bolt from the blue. A mystery solved.

"Alvirah's New York—from Pots to Plots."

She'd start the memoir this afternoon.

MADELINE

EDWIDGE DANTICAT

I WILL ALWAYS remember my first book. It was a used and frayed copy of Ludwig Bemelman's *Madeline*, given to me by my uncle, my father's brother, on my fourth birthday. It was in French, of course, Madeline's native tongue, and since I was living in Haiti at the time, it made perfect sense that I should be reading it that way.

Thirty years later, I can't recall the book's gentle Gallic rhymes as I had memorized them as a girl, but I can easily mouth them off in English (In an old house in Paris/That was covered with vines/Lived twelve little girls/In two straight lines . . .) as though this was the only language I'd ever known them in. Whether this is from extreme exposure to *Madeline* in English or a language shift memory lapse, I am not sure. However, much to my surprise, I later learned, when I moved to the United States from Haiti at age twelve, that Madeline's Austrian-born creator was a world traveler who divided his time between Paris and New York. In fact, as *française* as Madeline appeared (for what could be more French than a little girl named after Proust's beloved madelines), her story first came to life in New York City, on the back of menus at an eatery called Pete's Tavern.

Over the years, as I reflected on my experiences with Madeline—when I discovered her origins, it almost seemed as though she had followed me to New York—I realized how literary encounters, be they our first or last or most recent, can metamorphose over and over again, especially if one lives in New York.

I came to New York myself from Haiti in March 1981, not speaking any English. People often ask immigrants, especially wide-eyed children, what they find most impressive about New York when they start living here, and for me, one of the things that dazzled me most was the central branch of the Brooklyn Public Library. Having owned only one book, which I had to leave behind in Haiti for another child before boarding the plane to New York, I was amazed that any individual person or institution could possess more than a few, not to mention the thousands and thousands of volumes that lined the walls of the multistoried, majestic Grand Army Plaza building. On my first trip there, I was completely in awe and once I pulled myself away from the shelves, dazed with the possibility of a lifetime spent trying to read each and every book, I glanced across Eastern Parkway and spotted Grand Army Plaza's ornately detailed eighty-foot Civil War Memorial Arch, which looked an awful lot like the Arc de Triomphe that capped off the Champs-Elysées, images of which I had first seen in the Madeline books.

Had I suddenly landed in Paris? Had I slipped inside the pages of a Madeline book, like Alice in Wonderland? Or were these simply echoes of my reading life reverberating in my real one and vice versa?

Later I would borrow the Madeline books from that very same branch and compare Bemelman's drawings of Paris' Arc de Triomphe with the Grand Army Plaza arch. Both were magnificent creations, of course, but in my mind the Brooklyn arch won, hands down. It was simply a matter of reality trumping an image, even though I never would have had the appreciation I had for the Grand Army Plaza arch had I not first experienced one in Madeline's world.

I would also sit through the 1998 film interpretation of Madeline's adventures, starring a cherubic little girl named Hatty Jones and the Oscar-winner Frances McDormand as the eagle-eyed Miss Clavel. In the theater, I was surrounded by giggling children and their mothers, who seemed puzzled by my childless presence. In all that reading and movie watching, however, all I was seeking was that first thrill of being given a book, even one that had already been read by one or several other children, opening its pages and seeing in them a world so unlike my own that my jaw dropped and I sat still for hours trying to immerse myself in it.

As an aspiring writer, this is what I hoped to do, to create an experience for readers that would be like the one I'd first had with *Madeline*. But one's first book is a lot like one's first kiss. The thrill is not easy to duplicate, so I wrote, hoping to renew that sense of wonderment for myself—after all, what is a writer if not someone who has the front row seat to the story he or she is trying to tell?—stringing together each word out of sheer desperation to find out what happens next.

I probably would have not become a writer if I hadn't moved to New York. And maybe I wouldn't have become such a passionate reader at an early age had I not read *Madeline*. I grew up in a family of storytellers, whose everyday conversations were laced with proverbs, riddles, and song; however, no one seemed too concerned about recording the stories they told with the same ease as breathing. It was taken for granted that the spirited tales that burst out of my aunts and grandmothers would be carried into the future through us, their children and their children's children. Migration broke that chain and most of the children and grandchildren, nieces and nephews ended up moving to the United States, Canada, and some even to France, one to a tiny apartment in the shadow of the Arc de Triomphe.

As a new arrival in New York, I was grateful to rediscover a story I had enjoyed so much in another country, another language, at a different stage in my life. It went a long way in showing me that stories were not static, that characters evolved and traveled and could be made to speak different languages. And if Madeline could go to London and speak English, then why couldn't I live in Brooklyn and do the same? If this book could exist in several languages, maybe I could, too.

"Reading gives us someplace to go when we have to stay where we are," aphorist Mason Cooley said. But reading also gives us some place to stay when we have no choice but to go, when too much reality, like a dictatorship or economic hardship, is what we're trying to escape, a simple story, like a feisty little girl's misdeeds told in rhyme can feel like a soothing balm, one that offers retreat as well as solace. And with that simultaneous identification and separation, one is able to rewrite the book for oneself, heading off on the adventures it allows as well as one's own very real exploits. And even though we were as different as two little girls could possibly be, during one reading moment in time, Madeline was me and I was Madeline.

POSSIBILITIES UNLIMITED

KENNETH C. DAVIS

TWENTY-ONE YEARS OLD, halfway through college—and on a slow track to nowhere. Like many kids in my generation, I was not exactly "lost." I just didn't have anywhere to go. But I knew two things. I loved books and I wanted to be in New York.

Put it all together and that meant a job in a New York bookstore.

Born into the baby boom in suburban Westchester, I was the child of working class parents. My father drove trucks and my mother worked nights in a local office. While I had always loved books and reading, the notion of actually making a living as a writer never crossed my mind. As a boy, I delivered newspapers; I couldn't write for them!

It wasn't a question of thinking I had no talent. Instead, the concept of writing professionally simply did not exist for me. It was as foreign as being an astronaut or a gourmet chef.

After coasting though high school, I "stopped out" to work at a fast food joint. Peeling and frying 20-pound bags of onions quickly made me realize that school wasn't so terrible after all. I went to a small college near home, with a vague notion that I might teach some day. For two years, I savored college life, tinkering with writing courses and working on the school paper. I discovered that writing felt natural, but I still didn't know where I was going. Halfway through college, I "stopped out" again. Taking a job in a book warehouse, I found the bottom rung on the publishing ladder that ends with books in readers' hands. From there, it was a small step up the ladder to my bookstore job.

Working in a New York City bookstore was an arrival at a destination I didn't even know I was seeking. A bookstore job is an incredible education. And there is no question that once you get a taste of publishing, it can get in the bloodstream.

There is an exhilaration that comes from opening

that box of fresh books and seeing what a favorite writer has turned out. Or finding a dazzling new "no-name" talent who has everyone buzzing. Or coming across a childhood favorite you had forgotten. Meeting the publishing house sales reps who stopped in to show off their new lists was a glimpse into a world of ideas and culture and entertainment and politics all rolled into one. Browsing as I went, sampling writers I had never read, absorbing ideas. But more than just reading—inhaling the books around me.

Somewhere in there, I went back to college at night while working in the bookstore by day. And it was about that time that a coworker read some of my college papers.

"You shouldn't be selling books," she told me. "You should be writing them." (I swear it's true.) She was the same person who had told the bookstore owner to "Hire the kid" when I was being interviewed for the job. She was so smart, I eventually married her.

My future wife was also an aspiring journalist and eventually landed a job at the industry trade journal, *Publishers Weekly*. The world of books and publishers became our universe. I was soon freelancing for *PW* as well, writing "Forecasts" and eventually doing author features. Among my first articles were interviews with Norman Mailer and Gay Talese. To that kid in the bookstore, they were legends and I couldn't believe that this opportunity had come to me.

It was also around this time that New York Is Book Country made its opening splash. As a freelance writer, I covered that first event and I can still remember the excitement of strolling along a Fifth Avenue that had been cleared of cars and devoted to books.

Now I will confess: I am a New York snob with a view of the city somewhat akin to that famous Steinberg *New Yorker* drawing with New York City filling the foreground and an inconsequential rest of America on the other side of the Hudson. Being on Fifth Avenue with thousands of people who were "inhaling" those books was simply a confirmation: We were at the center of the universe!

A few years later, I returned to New York Is Book Country as a parent with a child in a backpack or a stroller or both. And now the allure of people dressed up as characters from our favorite children's books became the key attraction.

Looking back at those early years of New York Is Book Country, I know one thing: the notion that I would someday have books of my own displayed on Fifth Avenue was as alien to me as the concept of writing professionally had been just a few years earlier.

And that is the essence of what books and New York mean to me. Possibilities. Unlimited possibilities. It doesn't matter what you like to read—fiction, fantasy, classics, or cutting edge. The world of books and the world of New York come together to shout that in this place anything can happen. And that "over the rainbow" idea is what New York Is Book Country has become for me.

At the 2002 Book Country, I emerged from the subway at Fifty-third Street into this tsunami of the city's love for books, and was confronted by the sight of a three-booth display devoted to my *Don't Know Much About*® series. I stopped in my tracks. Goosebump time. The kid unpacking boxes of books twenty-five years earlier had arrived.

My teenage son was with me and I excitedly pointed the display out to him. He was—perhaps as only a seventeen-year-old son can be—completely underwhelmed. Reality check completed. I understood. He was my personal humility gauge. After all, some things never change.

LITERARY LANDMARK
NELSON DEMILLE

FTER THREE YEARS in the Army, I was discharged in April of 1969 and returned home to Long Island. During my one-year tour of duty in Vietnam, I'd met another Long Islander, Bob Reid, who was actually an Aussie, but who'd been living on Long Island when he somehow got drafted into the American Army.

Bob and I had both been infantry officers, serving in a frontline rifle company. He was the platoon leader of First Platoon, I was platoon leader of Second Platoon, and we saw a lot of action together.

In Vietnam, we'd made two promises to each other: The first was that we'd have a drink together when we got home; the second was that if one of us didn't go home, the other would visit the parents of the guy who didn't make it.

Fortunately, we both made it. Bob had been discharged before me and was already working in Manhattan by the time I got off the plane at JFK in April. He was into something called computer programming.

Bob and I made a date to have that drink, and he suggested La Maganette on Third Avenue, a place that's happily still there.

I met Bob at the bar about six P.M. Bob is taciturn and low key, so there was no hugging or effusiveness, just a brief handshake, as though we'd done this the night before. I ordered a Scotch. He was drinking a beer. Bob was wearing a suit, which shouldn't have surprised me, but the last time I'd seen him, he was wearing sweaty and muddy jungle fatigues. I, too, was wearing a suit, and I think we both thought we looked strange in mufti.

My head was still in the Army, but I could tell that Bob had made a successful and complete transition back to civilian life. We talked about the future and spoke not one word about Vietnam. Bob was the quintessential citizen-soldier who had done his duty to his adopted country and wanted neither praise for his service nor sympathy for his interrupted life.

Bob was dating an anesthesiologist who he said might join us for drinks later. We both drank, smoked, and checked out the after-work crowd. Fashions had changed in our absence, hair was longer for men and women, and a lot of the guys sported sideburns and bell bottoms. Attitudes had changed as well and returning veterans were not heroes. I think I still had an air of the military about me with my short hair and outdated suit. Bob's hair had grown, and his suit and tie looked a little more mod.

We moved from the bar to a table and ordered more drinks. I'd fantasized about being home, sitting in a bar in Manhattan in clean clothes with my life ahead of me. The reality matched the fantasy, maybe because the fantasy wasn't too extravagant and had consisted of nothing more than this, and having dinner with my parents and three brothers, which I'd already done.

I'd thought about calling an old girlfriend, which I hadn't done yet, and I'd thought about registering for the fall semester to complete my final year of college, but I hadn't done that either.

Some friends had rented a summer house in Southampton, Long Island, and they wanted two more guys to complete the arrangement. I asked Bob if he was interested, and he said, "Sure. Why not?"

As I said, Bob is not an effusive guy, and I noticed that I was not too effusive myself. In fact, I'd changed. I was no longer the happy and chatty college kid I'd been three years before, and the alcohol wasn't helping.

A Brooks Brothers kind of guy came over to the table and sat down. Bob was obviously expecting him and made a perfunctory introduction. The guy's name was John, and he and Bob had been roommates at Hamilton College.

John had been out of the Army about a year and was now working as an editor at a small publishing house. I took a liking to John—he drank, he smoked, he thought the war sucked, but also thought the anti-war crowd sucked.

The discussion turned to books, specifically war novels, such as Norman Mailer's *Naked and the Dead*, Erich Maria Remarque's *All Quiet on the Western Front*, and Hemingway's *Farewell to Arms*. Bob didn't have much to say, except he didn't read many novels and war novels probably sucked.

At that point in time, there were virtually no Vietnam War novels around, only some nonfiction, which none of us had read. The news was filled with the war, of course, and the war was still going on, and for that reason, according to John, he wasn't getting any fiction submissions about the war, which everyone was sick of anyway, and if he did get a Vietnam War novel, he wouldn't read it or publish it.

I suggested that, like the generations before us, the men who'd returned from the war would start to write about it and produce a great body of good and bad literature about the war.

John replied, "Maybe. But not for ten years. This war sucks."

The discussion turned predictably to women and stayed there. Bob's lady friend never showed up. No one suggested dinner, so we moved back to the bar and had a few nightcaps.

The next morning, I woke up with a hangover and an expanded fantasy. I wanted to be a writer, and I wanted to write about the subject that was barely mentioned the night before. The war.

I went out to Southampton in May and stayed until Labor Day, getting my head together. I returned to college, where the anti-war movement was in full swing, and I felt uncomfortable as an older student who'd spent three years in the Army.

I graduated, had a few unpleasant and unfulfilling jobs, and began writing paperback police novels on my kitchen table. John, with whom I had stayed in contact, published them, and I quit the day job and continued living my fantasy of being a writer, though the pay sucked.

I caught a few breaks, and in 1985, I finally wrote my Vietnam War novel, *Word of Honor*.

John and I and Bob have drifted apart, but now and then, I go back to La Maganette on Third Avenue and have a drink at the bar. If I'm with someone, that unlucky person has to hear about all of this, how three veterans got together one night and how we drank too much and how I decided that night, or maybe the next morning, to become a writer. Or maybe I decided much earlier and didn't know it until that night.

In any case, if you ever walk past La Maganette on Third Avenue, don't look for a brass plaque that says, "Nelson DeMille began his writing career here," but think of the thousands of writers whose careers began or flourished in the greatest literary city in the world. New York, New York.

READING FOR
THE FIRST TIME

PETE HAMILL

TWO YEARS AGO, deep into the writing of a novel, I started a project that will probably go on to the end of my days. My own novel was dense with history, much of it taking place in a New York that I had never seen. Research is obviously a stage in the writing of such a novel, but pure research is only the first step in the writing of a work of the imagination. The information—the facts—must have time to marinate, to mesh with dream, to move into imagined experience and memory. Among the many questions I had to answer about my main character was a simple one: what did he read?

That question launched me into the project that continues now, many months after the novel has been completed, set in type, bound, and shipped to book-stores.

Very simply it is this: I am reading books that I thought I had read when young, and I'm discovering that I'd never read them at all. It's a project of self-discovery, as thrilling to me as any voyage I've ever taken.

I started with *Don Quixote*, by Miguel de Cervantes. This was an appropriate choice, I thought, because the tale is certainly the first true novel, and remains one of the greatest ever written. All of my educated charac-ters would have read it in one form or another, and I had not opened it for more than thirty years. But I soon discovered that two people were now reading it, each bearing my name: the boy I was and the man I am. At some point in my Brooklyn childhood, I had vanished into the narrative of the illustrious don from La Man-cha and his skeptical, clear-eyed companion, Sancho Panza. There he was, up on Rosinante, wielding his battered lance as he went forth into the world on his missions of courage and chivalry. As a boy, I thought it was the funniest novel I'd ever read.

Now, in my sixth decade of life, Don Quixote fills me with enormous, grieving sadness. I keep saying to the knight: Don't listen to them, my illustrious don! You are right, and your sneering critics are wrong! Those are *not* windmills, they are *dragons!* And chivalry is not a romantic joke! The novel is, of course, wonderfully human, often comic, but informed by that most certain knowledge: each of us will die. And Quixote would rather die on his feet (or in the saddle of his steed) than collapse to his knees in fear and trembling. He is a true hero. And his creator is one of those rare literary geniuses whose work continues to feel as if it were written six months ago. This first novel accomplishes what more self-conscious modernists have done for decades now. In a way, its form is about itself; that is, the story is also about the telling of the story. At the same time, it proclaims the immense power of the human imagination.

The same is true of Dante's *Inferno*, which I read last year in the superb translation by Robert Pinsky. As a boy of eleven or twelve, a child of Catholic schools, I read this (or tried to read it) in a version borrowed from the Brooklyn Public Library. The edition contained the astonishing illustrations by Gustave Doré, which had drawn me to the book. For a few days, I entered the world of Dante Alighieri, into various levels of sin and punishment, and frankly, as an apprentice sinner, I was terrified. Whatever else might happen to me, I did not want to end up in Hell.

This time, the *Inferno* struck me as a sly, hilarious poem, at once a parody of church teaching, a vivid description of modern society (with all its invincible hypocrisies), and an ironical expression of human futility. Dante Alighieri knew something large: human folly never ends. But I read it, of course, as someone in my own time, not his, not even the time of the nineteenth century (when Doré made his terrifying pictures). And so I imagined Dante at a table in some city of exile, and John Gotti leaning in beside him, saying: "Don't figget the lawyizz. Put in about the lawyizz . . ." As if they were each in the witness protection program. And Dante smiling, nodding, and making a note to imagine some lines about the lawyers.

One other example: *Bleak House*, by Charles Dickens. The novel, published in 1852, was a century old when I read it as a kid in the Navy. For me, an eighteen-year-old from Brooklyn, *Bleak House* was a long, wordy detective story, and I turned the pages, wanting to know who had killed Mr. Tulkinghorn, and hoping that the detective, Mr. Bucket, would solve the mystery. The endless law case of Jarndyce vs. Jarndyce got in the way of the narrative, and I finished the novel through an act of will. After all, a year earlier I had graduated from the crude violence of Mickey Spillane to the high art of Raymond Chandler; as a detective story, *Bleak House* didn't seem worth the effort.

This time around, I was in awe of the shameless genius of Mr. Dickens. I don't use "shameless" casually. Dickens never walks away from the theatrical possibilities of a major scene; he always goes for what dancers call "the big mitt finish." At one point, for example, an important character (although not a major one) dies of spontaneous combustion. I mean, he just blows up. Dickens spends a few pages trying to make this plausible, but then he rushes on, plunging deeper into his story, deeper into his characters. It's a splendid ride, full of laughter, savage class criticism, the mysteries of "illegitimacy," examinations of good and evil and the spaces in between. When I finished it this time, I wanted to start reading it all over again.

The excitement of this project is not unique to me,

of course. I've mentioned my discoveries to some of my friends, and to strangers encountered at book signings, and they express the same astonishment. Yes, they say, the books we read while young are different when we read them a half century later. The reason is obvious: between readings, we've had our lives.

As writers from David Denby to Italo Calvino have said in other ways, the classics are books to which we can always return and be filled with the emotions of discovery. To read them is not to reject the newest works of high or popular literature. I usually alternate between a classic and a new work: Carl Hiaasen (our Jonathan Swift) can be read, absorbed, embraced between *Tom Jones* and *Treasure Island.* So can Elmore Leonard and Peter Blauner, Alan Furst and Kevin Baker, Stephen King and the Brooklyn works of my brother Denis Hamill. For me, the project is not some elaborate Great Books endeavor, driven by a need for "self-improvement," or some belated attempt to fill in intellectual blanks. It's rooted in a determination to make those older books a vivid part of the present tense of my life, rather than mere way stations of my youth.

We do this in all the other arts, too. Tupac Shakur

did not erase Duke Ellington, J. S. Bach, or Erik Satie, and Norah Jones will not send Billie Holiday to the trash can. We can laugh with Steve Martin without obliterating the Marx Brothers. We can marvel at the paintings of Richard Diebenkorn without slamming the doors on Diego Velázquez. All can be part of the amazing richness of a single human life.

For those of us who have lived long lives, those great works are also a consolation. Too many things vanish in life: parents, friends, beloved dogs, intimate streets, night places, ballparks. But for as long as we live, no matter where we wander, we can always go back to *Madame Bovary*, or *Ulysses*, or *Leaves of Grass*, or *Absalom, Absalom*. We can find new marvels in Machado de Assis or Lady Murusaki or Lord Byron. We can spend a cold New York evening on the Pequod, hunting the white whale. We can swagger through a weekend with D'Artagnan or Scaramouche, be illuminated by Tolstoy or Dostoyevsky or Chekov, sing with Yeats or Heaney. And yes: we can sail with Odysseus, knowing that the point is not simply to go forth into the scary world, but to find a way home.

MEMORIES OF NEW YORK CITY SNOW

OSCAR HIJUELOS

F OR IMMIGRANTS of my parents' generation,
who had first come to New York City from the
much warmer climate of Cuba in the mid-1940s, the
very existence of snow was a source of fascination. A
black-and-white photograph that I have always loved,
circa 1948, its surface cracked like that of a thawing
ice-covered pond, features my father, Pascual, and my
godfather, Horacio, fresh up from Oriente Province,
posing in a snow-covered meadow in Central Park.
Decked out in long coats, scarves, and black-brimmed
hats, they are holding, in their be-gloved hands, a huge
chunk of hardened snow. Trees and their straggly
witch's hair branches, glimmering with ice and frost,
recede into the distance behind them. They stand on a

field of whiteness, the two men seemingly afloat in midair, as if they were being held aloft by the magical substance itself.

That they bothered to have this photograph taken—I suppose to send back to family in Cuba—has always been a source of enchantment for me. That something so common to winters in New York would strike them as an object of exotic admiration has always spoken volumes about the newness—and inno-cence—of their immigrants' experience. How thrilling it all must have seemed to them, for their New York was so very different from the small town surrounded by farms in eastern Cuba that they hailed from. Their New York was a fanciful and bustling city of endless sidewalks and unimaginably high buildings; of great bridges and twisting outdoor elevated train trestles; of walkup tenement houses with mysteriously dark basements, and subways that burrowed through an underworld of girded tunnels; of dancehalls, burlesque houses, and palatial department stores with their com-plement of Christmastime Salvation Army Santa Clauses on every street corner. Delightful and perilous, their New York was a city of incredibly loud noises, of police and air raid sirens and factory whistles and subway rumble; a city where people sometimes shushed you for speaking Spanish in a public place, or could be unforgiving if you did not speak English well or seemed to be of a different ethnic background. (My father was once nearly hit by a garbage can that had been thrown off the rooftop of a building as he was walking along La Salle Street in upper Manhattan.)

Even so, New York represented the future. The city meant jobs and money. Newly arrived, an aunt of mine went to work for Pan Am; another aunt, as a Macy's saleslady. My own mother, speaking nary a word of English, did a stint in the garment district as a seamstress. During the war some family friends, like my godfather, were eventually drafted, while others ended up as factory laborers. Landing a job at the Biltmore Men's Bar, my father joined the hotel and restaurant workers' union, paid his first weekly dues, and came home one day with a brand new white chef's toque in hand. Just about everybody found work, often for low pay and ridiculously long hours. And while the men of that generation worked a lot of overtime, or a second job, they always had their day or two off. Dressed to the hilt, they'd leave their uptown neighborhoods and make an excursion to another part of the city—

perhaps to one of the grand movie palaces of Times Square or to beautiful Central Park, as my father and godfather, and their ladies, had once done, in the aftermath of a snowfall.

Snow, such as it can only fall in New York City, was not just about the cold and wintry differences that mark the weather of the north. It was about a purity that would descend upon the grayness of its streets like a heaven of silence, the city's complexity and bustle abruptly subdued. But as beautiful as it could be, it was also something that provoked nostalgia; I am certain that my father would miss Cuba on some bitterly cold days. I remember that whenever we were out on a walk and it began to snow, my father would stop and look up at the sky, with wonderment—what he was seeing I don't know. Perhaps that's why to this day my own associations with a New York City snowfall have a mystical connotation, as if the presence of snow really meant that some kind of inaccessible divinity had settled his breath upon us.

A WRITER IN
THE VILLAGE

bell hooks

N O MATTER WHERE he traveled in the world,
no matter that he chose to live in exile, James
Baldwin was quintessentially a New York writer. All
Baldwin's work, whether essay or novel, in some way
referenced New York. When, as a young man, he made
his break with home and family in Harlem, the first
place of exile he chose was Greenwich Village. Leaving
Harlem for the bohemian art world of the Village,
Baldwin declared: "I had to jump then or I would quite
simply have died." The Village of Baldwin's day was
the place of transgression and possibility. It was the
subculture where artists and writers, privileged class
exiles and runaways, came to nurture their creativity.
At the White Horse Tavern and all around the Village,

Baldwin met fellow bohemians (the Beat poets Jack Kerouac and Allen Ginsberg, the young actor Marlon Brando, Paul Robeson, Claude McKay, Margaret Mead); finding in this new world passions that moved him beyond the categories of race, gender, and sexual preference into a world where artists were focusing on transcending categories and finding in that transcendence unifying visions.

In the small towns where I have lived most of my life whenever I imagined living in New York I conjured a vision of readers and books, of artists and writers, a world of late-night conversation, of feverish intense words spilling out of the mouth and onto the page. It comforted me to imagine that I was dreaming about a New York that was no more. Nostalgia about the Village back then made me feel secure as a writer, not "left out" because I had no New York literary experience, no sense of existing in a world of artistic temperament where the drive to create and revel in creation was all around thick in the very air one breathed. I knew then (or so I believed) that I would never live in New York; my thoughts about the city were purely the stuff of small-town fantasy. But, like all absolute knowing, life proved me wrong.

My thinking about New York was changed by a visit by a New York–based artists collective, Group Material, that came to the local museum to give a talk (Andre Serrona, Julie Ault, and Felix Gonzales Torres to name a few). Interracial, gay and straight, poor and privileged, they brought big apple cool to a small town. Julie and I bonded from the moment we met. A reader of my books, she heard that I lived in this small town and wanted to meet me so she asked around. Most people she talked to told her "no one by that name lives here." With New York bloodhound intensity, Julie called folks in the city to get my number. And when she arrived at my house on Elm Street, the first thing she said was, "You don't belong here—you gotta move to New York. You're like a hidden treasure here. These people, they don't even know your name. You gotta get out." She opened the door. "Come visit. Come meet people." And so I came to New York. She lived in the Village. And like the bohemians of the past, the cafés and clubs near her flat were places where we gathered to talk and share ideas.

When I moved to New York I came to Greenwich Village because I wanted to be part of that tradition of writers flocking here to find lost parts of themselves.

Unlike Baldwin, I came to the Village as an already
"known" writer. It took living in New York City to let
me know how well known my work was. If no one
recognized me in the small town I had been dwelling
in, I was initially stunned that so many people walked
up to me in the city and said, "Are you bell hooks? I've
read . . ." That was really the way New York seduced
me. It revealed itself to me as a city of readers. Since
much of my life revolves around reading and writing,
coming to live in the city, in the Village, seemed like a
dream come true. Here I was living right near a jazz
club and meeting Amiri and Amina Baraka, and talking about life for the writer in the Village then
and now.

Many of us writers who live in the Village are pros-
perous, and while we aspire to the wild heady bohemian spirits of the past, mostly we work a lot. All
around me I feel surrounded by the spirits of writers
and thinkers from the past (some living, most dead)
whose work still lives for me. Thomas Merton, Eudora
Welty, Norman Mailer, Jack Kerouac. When I come out
of my flat I am likely to occasionally run into Stanley
Crouch, conservative, critic (he's had a biting comment
to make now and then about bell hooks), and good

neighbor. Underneath the don't-get-next-to-me façade is a writer and thinker who likes to talk, to work it. And so we have sat down in places in our hood we frequent and let the words fly, loud and lively. We like meeting this way spontaneously, no planned assignation, no planned topic, just letting loose with all the ideas rumbling around in our heads. Or when I first met Michael Cunningham and talked with him about writing, about *The Hours* when it was the book and only the book.

Mostly I spend my time with beloved comrade and friend Roni Horn, an artist whose work continues to take me to new places. She is, like me, a Village girl through and through; we like to stay close to home, stay in hour hood, we like quiet evenings of good food, intense talks, and great music. We like to read. Our homes are full of books. It seems to be a Village thing. Outside our small flats we run into readers—we talk books.

Tracy (long-time bookseller at Three Lives, passed away) was part of our reading crew. She was an old time lesbian, a Southern white girl who had been everywhere and seen it all. Yet she was always lured back to the world of the Village, to the readers she cultivated and nurtured. She would save for us the right book—the book she thought we needed to read. I miss her and all she stands for in life and death—a world of openness, of beloved community, of life lived beyond the categories of race, class, gender, sexual preference, a world where books and ideas are the meeting place, the foundation of connection and community.

Books and bookstores are all around our neighborhood. In New York City reading is one of the fun things to do—there is no other nation where reading, writing, and talking about books is so commonplace. And if you are lucky—lucky to be living here in book country, or just passing through—you might find a small stack of books on a stoop, or in a box on the sidewalk waiting for you. Books someone is giving away. It happens; I need a particular book, I take a walk and someone has set it there for me to find. Only in book country—it's the place where I belong.

TELLING THE STORIES
WADE HUDSON

WHEN I WAS GROWING UP in the segregated South in the 1950s and 1960s, books were an important part of my world. I read everything: biographies, novels, essays. Books allowed me to look outside my small, provincial town in Louisiana. Although I felt protected and cared for by my family and my community (which was a difficult challenge in segregated Louisiana), I knew a different world awaited me. This world, though filled with its own challenges, was where I would find my place. Books helped me to understand that place.

Books took me places I could never go physically. In books I met people who were famous and those who lived ordinary lives. Books allowed me to travel into the past and take adventurous sojourns into the future. They helped me better understand the world in which I lived. They liberated me. They helped me feel good about myself. They let me know that I was important even when others around me told me that I was not. Books became some of my best friends.

My world of books was not all rosy. Not many of the books I read featured African Americans as characters. Those that did often portrayed us as pathetic creatures with very little to offer society. But I was able to cut my way through the vines and the undergrowth that sometimes hid the humanity. It was there, where the humanity laid bare, that I could identify with the characters and the stories and find myself. Humanity is the place where we all connect, and where we all find our being. The vines and the undergrowth are what we use to cover it up, to hide it.

The more books I read, the more I realized that our stories, our history, had to be told. I was not aware of Richard Wright, Ralph Ellison, Langston Hughes, or Gwendolyn Brooks. I had never heard of the Harlem Renaissance or Paul Laurence Dunbar. But I had this burning desire to one day tell our stories. I wanted to give people the opportunity to see the glory and majesty of our experiences as African Americans, as well as the pain and the anguish. So I set out to tell our stories. And along the way I learned that many other blacks had sat down, pen in hand, to tell our stories, too. Many had done so decades before my humble attempts.

My life's journey has taken many twists and turns. But books and the desire to tell our stories have always been constant, whether with poems, plays, essays, or songs.

In 1988, my wife, Cheryl, and I started a children's publishing company, Just Us Books. We recognized the need not only to tell our stories but to publish them as well to affirm our history and culture for children. We also knew how important it was for children, particularly black youngsters, to see children who look like them in the books they read.

We located our company in the New York metropolitan area, home of the book publishing industry, where many established writers and artists live and thrive. New York is noted for its racial and ethnic diversity and its many forums that allow for a wide range of voices to be heard. Cultural, art, and music institutions seem to be everywhere. But as we made plans to launch our company, these important factors were not paramount. Rather, we thought about *Freedom's Journal*, the first

black newspaper, and its first editorial written by Samuel
Cornish and John Russwurm in 1827. "We wish to plead
our own case," it read. "Too long has the publick been de-
ceived by misrepresentations, in things which concern us
dearly.

We thought about the words of Langston Hughes, a
giant of the Harlem Renaissance. In an essay entitled
"The Negro Artist and the Racial Mountain," Harlem's
adopted son wrote: "We younger Negro artists who create now intend to express our individual dark-skinned
selves without fear or shame . . . We build our temples for
tomorrow, strong as we know how, and we stand on top of
the mountain, free within ourselves." We thought about
the Schomburg Center for Research in Black Culture,
and we knew we could utilize its great collection of
books, photographs, manuscripts, films, and recordings.
We thought about many other important events, people,
and places in African-American history that have New
York City connections. We knew we were in the right
place to launch our company.

We celebrated our fifteenth year in publishing in
2003. Just as *Freedom's Journal*, the Harlem Renaissance, and the Schomburg Center have made an
impact on society, we know Just Us Books has, too.

ME AND MY HOOTEN

EVAN HUNTER

W E DIDN'T HAVE TELEVISION when I was a boy growing up in New York. We had the window. In the summertime, my mother used to open the window in my bedroom and she would put a pillow on the windowsill, and I would place my elbows on the pillow and look down into the street from six stories up, and that was my television.

This was 120th Street between First and Second Avenues.

It was a busy street.

We used to have dinner early because my father was a mailman who got up at four-thirty in the morning so he could get to the post office on time to sort the mail before he went out to deliver it. By six at night, he was

ready for a good meal. I would go downstairs after dinner (we called it supper, I remember) and play with the
other little kids on the block until it started getting
dark, and then my mother would yell down from the
window, "Honey, come on up now!" and I'd climb the
six flights up to our railroad flat—that's an apartment
without hallways, one room just leads into the other—
and go into my bedroom and lean on the pillow and
watch the street as the softness of a summer night
claimed it.

There were hundreds of stories on that street.

More than you can find on all the television chan-
nels today.

Private telephones weren't common in that part of
Harlem. There was a pay phone in the candy store
downstairs from our building, and everyone on the
block would leave that number as his own. The owner
of the store would answer the phone and then send
whichever kid was hanging around to go get whomever
the call was for. The recipient was supposed to tip you
a nickel or a dime and you had to spend that in the candy store. From my window, I could hear the phone
ringing in the candy store. I could see kids in knickers
running into this or that apartment building and com-

ing back out with a man or a woman, sticking close so he'd get his tip. I used to wonder what all those phone calls were about. I used to make up stories about those phone calls.

When I was twelve, we moved to the Bronx and got our own telephone. This was because my father became a "regular" as opposed to a "substitute" mailman, which he'd been all through the Depression. Because we were now rich, my mother gave me two cents every night after dinner, to go buy candy at the store up on Bronxwood Avenue. I didn't even have to hang around the telephone to get the two cents. She just gave it to me. We lived on 217th Street, between Barnes and Bronxwood Avenues. I would stroll up past the ice station on the corner, and then make a right turn, and walk into the candy store and tell the proprietor I would like a Two-Cent Hooten, please, which was this thick chocolate bar, either with or without nuts. Then I would walk down Bronxwood to 216th Street, and come around past Olinville Junior High, eating my chocolate bar, and hoping I wouldn't run into any friends who might want a bite.

One summer night after dinner, I was strolling up to Bronxwood to buy my Hooten, when all at once there was a commotion in the streets. A kid I knew yelled, "Come on!" and I raced up to Bronxwood Avenue with him, and while we were running up to 219th Street, I asked what was going on. He said, "It's a fight! Grab a stick! Come on!"

I grabbed a stick.

There were hundreds of kids on the avenue, running toward each other.

All at once I was face to face with a kid I didn't know, and he had a stick in his hand, too, and suddenly we were hitting each other with the sticks, and I thought *Huh?*

I threw the stick away.

I turned around and walked right back to 217th Street, past the ice station on the corner, and I walked into the candy store and told the proprietor I would like a Two-Cent Hooten, please.

I still don't know what that fight was about.

THERE'S A LIGHT
ON IN BROOKLYN

SUSAN ISAACS

A D M I R E my author-pals who write their memoirs:
Tony Hillerman, Patricia Volk, Mary Higgins Clark.
No, the truth is I envy them. Wow, to clutch your past
in your hand! To turn it this way, then that, see every
aspect of your family's life, observe your friends, your
teachers, and, the most riveting character of all, yourself. To hold that past up and . . . Yes! Dialogue from
decades earlier.

My memoir would have a lot of blank pages. My
past isn't a crystal with hundreds of facets or a straight
line with thousands of teeny perpendiculars that indi-
cate "entered first grade wearing blue dress with puffy
sleeves that made her look like a milkmaid from a
Baltic republic." My life cannot be a memoir. Instead,

it seems a series of random incidents from a thick book with many blank pages.

Okay, here are a couple of the episodes—about me and books.

On late winter afternoons in Brooklyn, a floor lamp shone on the dark hair of my mother's lowered head. No spotlight, no vanity. The light was on to illuminate the pages of whatever book she was reading. What a sight! Matron in a Circle of Light, stark, dramatic. Definitely not a comedy.

The rest of the apartment remained unlit until a few minutes before my father, an electrical engineer, was due home. The darkness might have been to save a few cents on the Con Ed bill—the Depression mentality enduring long after the 1930s were history. More likely, it was my mother's own depression. To get up and turn on the lights would have meant pulling herself out of the universe of whatever novel she was reading and looking at the life she actually had.

Where was I in all this darkness? I haven't a clue. Maybe observing, like a good little novelist-in-training. (I was not, however, one of those sensitive kids who kept a journal and recorded every flutter of a butterfly's wings. The only childhood literary aspiration I recall came later, when at ten or eleven I longed to be sophisticated enough to write dirty limericks. But as a younger child, my sole career goal, beside the compulsory dream to get married, was to be a cowgirl, which should tell you something about my own relationship with reality.)

More likely, I came home from school, said "Hi" to the woman in the circle of light and offered an amusing vignette of my day at P.S. 197. If there hadn't been a diverting incident, I made one up. She loved these little stories. They brought a smile and, occasionally, a chuckle. They reassured her that I was having a happy childhood. Post-vignette, I suppose, I grabbed a couple of Mallomars and went off to play with friends with higher wattage mothers.

Still, the remembrance of my mother in her chair, rocking slowly with Edna Ferber and James Michener, speeding up for Daphne du Maurier and Herman Wouk, was indelible. During those times, she was transported to another place where I sensed she was leading a much better life. That's what I wanted, too. As soon as I could read full sentences, in second grade, she gave me what she considered the best possible gift, a library card.

These days, I'm not sure precisely where that branch of the Brooklyn Public Library is, or was. My mental map puts it in deepest Flatbush, on Ocean Avenue and Avenue P. For all I know, it may have been as gloomy as Hades inside, but my mental picture (which overlays my mental map) is of a high-ceilinged, luminous place. Starry pinpoints of light reflected off the protective plastic covers on the books. Objectively, I know the plastic was cloudy with finger-prints and sneezes and tacky from the caked-on residue of Truman-Eisenhower era fast food—cinnamon toast, canned Elberta cling peaches. Big deal: They gleamed to me.

Okay, the bad news about me and books: No one suggested, "Hey, kid, check out *The Secret Garden* or *Little Women*." Other children's classics were hardly ever mine because I didn't know about them. The ones I did read fell into my hands not through any guidance, but because there were multiple copies on the library shelves and thus pathetically available. I came across *Heidi*, read it, and added the novel to my overlong "creepy" list, along with *Alice in Wonderland, Hansel and Gretel*, clowns, soft-boiled eggs, subway tunnels, and so forth. The only book revered by people with exquisite sensibilities that I can remember enjoying was *Black Beauty*. Any darkness in it was overt, in the color of the horse and the horror of its mistreatment. None of that inner darkness business for me.

By fourth grade, I meandered out of the children's section and was free to choose any book I could reach. The good news? My mother was thrilled by my love of books and came through for me. A note from her let me check out more than the allotted two per kid per week. She knew two books for seven days were child's play for a girl who'd inherited the reading gene.

So I'd lumber home down Ocean Avenue, parallel with the trolley tracks, with five to ten books about my current interest: dinosaurs, Tudor England, rodeos, astronomy. I read indiscriminately, fiction and nonfiction: *Gone With the Wind, Auntie Mame, How to Win Friends and Influence People, Tallulah, The Sea Around Us, Anne Frank, Diary of a Young Girl, East of Eden.* To this day I am still transported heavenward by the sour smell of library books.

Even more than my elementary school vignettes, my mother took pleasure in having me recount each book I read. I would switch on all the lamps, sit in a club chair facing her rocker, and be the grownup recit-

ing a story to an utterly captivated child, the star entertaining an enthralled audience.

Another page from my biography, a much later one.
I dropped over my mother's apartment. Dark. As
always, I flicked on all the lights. The books I'd given
her, along with novels I'd written (and their transla-
tions) filled the shelves behind her. She was sitting in
her rocking chair, but not reading. Something was
wrong. Well, I suppose the word should be wronger.
"Mom, do you want me to take you to the library?" She
shook her head. "Well, tomorrow I'll bring over a
bunch of books for you."

"No."

"No?"

"I don't want to read," she said. As I was asking why
not, she cut me off. "I don't like to read anymore."

The next day I took out some books on Alzheimer's.

BOOK VS. BOOK
IN QUEENS

ROBERT LIPSYTE

MY FATHER AND I didn't go to ballgames; we went to the library. The scrubby little Rego Park branch of the Queens Borough Public Library was our local sandlot. The vast, grand, stone building of the Elmhurst branch was our Yankee Stadium.

Almost every week Dad drove me, and later my kid sister, too, to Elmhurst. I was allowed to take out as many books as I could carry, which explains my present upper body strength if not my overload of free-floating information.

It was at Elmhurst, choosing books and talking about them with Dad, that I came to realize that books, like people, are good and bad, and sometimes both. I learned that there were books to love and books to trust and books to use without necessarily having to love or trust or even judge them.

I learned that books lead to books. If I hadn't discovered Steinbeck as a child in Elmhurst, I would never have gotten to Gordimer as an adult in Manhattan. From Mary Renault to Dawn Powell to Hari Kunzru, from John R. Tunis to Salinger, Roth, Updike, and everybody else I read outside of school.

I also learned that books can be dangerous and that books can save you.

It was at Elmhurst that I was set upon by a vicious bully of a book. I reeled with that destructive confusion that seems hopelessly dark, even deadly, in early adolescence.

I was rescued by a dashing hero of a book with a twinkle in his eye.

The bad book, which I think had a mouse gray cover, was in the Science section, where I often trolled for sex education. It was called *The New You and Heredity*. I thought I spotted some instructive anatomical pictures, so I stuck the book in the middle of my pile and flashed it at my father, who nodded routinely. I was allowed to take out anything the librarians would lend me.

The bad book, read under covers by flashlight, turned out to be boring until I found the masculinity chart.

Atop the chart were test pilots and engineers. At the bottom were teachers, librarians, and writers. I didn't know anything about junk science in those days, only that the words in a book were probably true. There was no question in my mind that I was going to be a writer, if not a teacher or librarian. I was headed for the bottom of the chart if I wasn't there already. Just when I was wondering when I would become a real man, I had scientific proof it would never happen.

I wanted to talk to Dad about it, but he was a teacher. I didn't want to make him feel bad, too. I considered him manly; I knew the inner city kids he taught thought so. He had muscles and a no-nonsense manner. But it was in a book.

Even now, as an ancient sports scribe who has seen just how fragile the "manliness" of our hyped heroes is, I cannot find amusement in that long-gone boy's terrible week of uncertainty. The battle of boyhood is hard enough without bad books. Youth may well be wasted on the young, but too often it wastes them. That book may have been one of the reasons why a dozen years later I started writing novels for teenagers.

The following Saturday when we went back to Elmhurst I returned that hateful *The New You and Heredity*, and plunged down lanes of bookcases in search of its antidote.

It must have been the great god of books, call it Skoob, who led me to a section I had rarely visited— Travel—and right to *The Royal Road to Romance*, by Richard Halliburton, a writer I had never read.

I think of that book in vivid reds, yellows, and blues.

Richard Halliburton wandered the world armed with the deadliest of weapons, a portable typewriter. The story in his book that thrilled me most began with Halliburton's frantic swim across a crocodile-infested river a few strokes ahead of unfriendly natives. His typewriter was strapped to his back, his Bowie knife gripped in his teeth. Somewhere in mid-stream, he had to defend himself against a cranky croc. A few minutes later, the makings of a handbag in his pocket, he reached shore, unslung the typewriter and pounded out the tale I re-read for so many nights I had to pay an overdue fine.

It was worth it to swagger back to science and snarl, "Okay, Mr. New You, just put Halliburton on the bottom of your masculinity chart and he'll carve you a new frontispiece if I don't do it first."

I casually mentioned the two books to Dad. He rolled his eyes and with a wave dismissed them both.

That was about fifty years ago. My dad is ninety-nine now. We still talk mostly about books. He roams his suburban New York county hunting books at flea markets, church basements and library sales. He lives in a house crammed with books double and triple tiered, perilously near avalanche. Not as many as stacked in Elmhurst, but probably as many as in the old Rego Park Branch. He urges his books on me, my sister, his grandkids; we can borrow as many as we can carry.

For years, I've had Dad on red alert for *The New You and Heredity* and *The Royal Road to Romance* but they have yet to show up in his used book bazaars. I wonder if they are such treasures that people never let them go. Or has Skoob spirited away all copies for the good of boykind? Best of all, most comforting, is the fantasy that in the process of becoming a writer I just made them up.

TO THE VISITOR:
A BENT EAR,
A COCKED EYE

FRANK MCCOURT

VISITORS FORCE YOU to think. They arrive with that helpless do-with-me-what-you-will look and when you ask what they'd like to do or see they say, "Oh, what's good?"

What's good? In New York?

You tell them—gently—that this is New York where everything is good. Everything, baby. Example: sitting on any park bench eavesdropping on two senior citizens discussing enemas is good. Gawking at lovers rolling in the Sheep Meadow of Central Park is good.

Visitors will say, "Oh, wait a minute. Hold on. I mean, these are two activities that are almost illegal, eavesdropping and gawking."

You respond, "If you live in a New York apartment

you are, willy-nilly, an eavesdropper and a gawker. Noises and conversations seep through walls, and what are you to do when people across the way simply won't pull down their blinds?"

You could go on—and you do. You try to describe the little things that bring so much satisfaction to the native—or resident—New Yorker. There are moments of exquisite pleasure the visitor could never appreciate.

A bialy with a schmeer is good, especially if you're on the Lower East Side. Visitors will be dismissive: "Oh, you can get that in L.A." You can feel only pity for such ignorance when everyone knows a bialy made beyond the borders of New York is Styrofoam.

A hot dog with everything eaten standing up at Nathan's in Coney Island is good.

A westward walk on the Brooklyn Bridge when the sun is setting in New Jersey is good.

A ride on the Staten Island ferry at sunset when the sky is a golden backdrop to the Statue of Liberty and Ellis Island is very good. A subway train rattles into the station. There's a surge of riders to the doors and the conductor's voice is heard, "Let 'em off, please. Let 'em off." You've learned how to dance your way through the passengers while the conductor requests everyone to, "Use all the doors, please. Use all the doors." When you skip nimbly to that vacant seat and secure it you try not to look too smug about your little triumph. You thought fleetingly of offering the seat to an elderly person but you're only going a few stops and you'll give it up in a minute.

You have to live in the city a long time before you can appreciate these moments and there's no use in trying to explain them to visitors. Your job is to find "what's good" and lead them to it.

Culture is what you think you have to think about when helpless visitors announce their impending arrival, but there are other types of visitors. Only the very enterprising will have an idea of what they want to do during their stay. By dawn's early light they're up and out of the house, leaving a made-up bed that would delight a marine corps drill sergeant. You'll find them at a coffee shop around the corner sharing an organic muffin and planning the day's activities with the help of map, guide, and what's going on in the newspapers. They leave daily notes describing the plays they saw, Broadway, off and off-off, cutting edge and classical. They check in from time to time to tell you of a cute little Korean restaurant they've discovered in Flushing, which you can get to on the number 7 train. They're breathless over the stimulating exhibits in galleries and museums you've always meant to visit yourself, the exquisite little inexpensive restaurants they discovered (all by themselves!) in crooked little Greenwich Village alleyways that you must MUST visit and it would be their pleasure to invite you out some night if they can find a moment (so much to do in New York, so little time). You've been such a wonderful host and maybe they'll see you tonight for a little wine before bed? And they bring you villainous pastries from Little Italy that replace all the carbohydrates you denied yourself for the past six months.

Efficient visitors like these are of no use to the gracious host and should be encouraged next time to find a budget hotel. They breeze in and out and the way they "do" the city in five days leaves you feeling ignorant and irrelevant.

Gratefully, you turn to those who need you—the helpless. You are challenged by their innocence, a manifestation of your own. You ask yourself, "If I were visiting New York for the first time what would I want to see or do?"

There are images: the Empire State Building, the

Brooklyn Bridge, the skyline in general, Fifth Avenue, Rockefeller Center with the skating rink and Atlas out there supporting the world, St. Patrick's Cathedral, Macy's, Orchard Street, Chinatown, Little Italy—all there for the gawking.

Museums? Don't be such a phony. You're a New Yorker and we know that if museums depended on the visits of New Yorkers they'd be crumbling by Christmas.

But they're good for the children. The little ones need the culture and what's the use of living in the city if we don't expose them to culture?

Ladies and gentlemen, please, please don't invoke the children, especially when it concerns museums. A hoary trick. There are millions of New Yorkers, dead and alive, who never set foot inside a museum and lived happy normal lives to the end.

If your visitors want to trot off to the Metropolitan Museum of Art, the Museum of the City of New York, the Museum of Modern Art, the American Natural History Museum, stand not in their way.

No, you can't do that to your helpless visitors. Take a few days off from whatever you're doing. Take your visitors by the hand. Sit on a park bench and smell the pigeons. Eavesdrop. Gawk. Stroll down or up Broadway to Times Square and dig those lights, oh those lights. Get half price tickets and see a show. Find a street vendor and have a hot dog with everything. It's not Coney Island, it's just Times Square and who in the world hasn't dreamed of Times Square?

Pay no attention to time or to people warning you New York isn't safe. Walk down Broadway, all the way down to Bowling Green. Watch people lining up for the ferry to Ellis Island and the Statue of Liberty. Just look at the people. Look. It's not gawking. You're looking at the country's history and if that's a gawk, so be it. And listen to them in their various tongues. You're not eavesdropping. You're listening to generations and to yourself.

And all that is good.

ON READING

GITA MEHTA

S OME TIME AGO I accepted an invitation to address a benefit in San Francisco for the National
Kidney Foundation, and attend their annual fundrais-
ing banquet. Since the year was 1997, the state California, and the banquet held in one of the grandest houses
on Nob Hill, many captains of Silicon Valley companies
were also present. Indeed, some of them were seated at
my table, animatedly discussing total velocity and
mythic sums of money. When the conversation finally
turned general, a young president of a high technology
corporation leaned toward me, "I'm afraid I haven't
read your books. But I don't know anyone who reads
books anymore. We get anything we want on the Internet."

At that point there was a lull in the chatter, so he had the attention of the entire table when he enquired kindly, as if speaking to someone in an old folks' home, "Actually, can you give me a good reason why I should read a book again?"

Actually, no, I couldn't. In a brave new world of virtual reality, I wasn't about to try and make a case for imagined reality. Virtual or otherwise, T. S. Eliot had once observed that humankind cannot take too much reality, and what the chairman of the Federal Reserve was calling "irrational exuberance" would soon give way to sobriety. But tonight time was running in nanoseconds. Multibillion dollar fortunes were waiting to be made. Futurists were hurtling down the information highway toward a very literal utopia where Tolstoy and Plato, Bach and Shakespeare, Da Vinci and Dante were little more than dead white men. It hardly seemed the moment to recommend reading novels as a means of comprehending human experience. Or to suggest poetry might prove useful when the literal exploded into the unthinkable.

Five years later, on a brilliant September morning in New York, the unthinkable occurred.

From a downtown Manhattan shrouded in debris

and smoke from fires that would take three months to quench, artists and writers unable to leave their homes were using the Internet to alert each other to a poem that might offer some consolation against the senseless carnage.

Farther north at Union Square, the message had come off the computers and was being written in felt nib pens on sheets of blank paper taped around the square, a tabula rasa on which a bereaved city could leave its messages.

Among the rare customers who ventured into the uptown book stores, some were looking for the same text that had been emailed from downtown or scribbled on the pavements at Union Square, drawn by the frightening precision of the lines.

"The unmentionable odour of death

Offends the September night."

Like so many others reading W. H. Auden's "September 1, 1939" in those weeks, I found it hard to believe the poem had been written half a century earlier. The words were too accurate, too descriptive of the rage and anguish evoked by the badly printed fliers with the faces of missing strangers that plastered the city, "obsessing our private lives."

In a metropolis shocked into silence, every activity seemed paralyzed by the universal inability to understand why. Ignorance made our fears more painful, as if reinforcing the truth of Elias Canetti's observation, "The act of naming is the great and solemn consolation of mankind."

The act of naming is among the strongest argument for reading books, an argument that has been made often during the course of human history. In India, it first appears in a story told about India's oldest extant text, the *Rig Veda*.

The way this story goes, in the very early days of the universe, when all is cloaked in ignorance, a mother has a son, a great and powerful bird called Garuda. The son grows up and his mother tells him the time has come for him to go out into the universe where he will face many terrible obstacles. If he overcomes them all, he will acquire a wonderful prize.

So Garuda travels through the cosmos confronting angry gods and fearful monsters, but each encounter has a terrifying immediacy. Although he has immense physical power, he has no knowledge of time or space or phenomena to permit him to connect one event to another, and like a monstrous drunk he staggers through the universe, blindly overcoming the challenges that are out before him until he finally gains the prize.

The prize is only a book, the *Rig Veda*. Disappointed, a weary Garuda perches upon a tree and he starts to read. To his astonishment, he finds in this book the names, narratives, emotions, tenses, characteristics, causes, and histories of his experiences: a code through which he can relate one time, one being, one thing to another. And, more important, to himself.

It is said in Indian mythology that for an entire epoch Garuda does not once raise his head from the pages of the book. A similar prospect may well face us all. Microprocessing technology is moving so rapidly soon every book in the world will be contained in a chip smaller than the head of a pin. Biotechnology may even make it possible to have that chip embedded in our heads.

Carrying the library of Alexandria in our pockets or in our frontal lobes is an awe-inspiring thought. Alas, possession is not synonymous with comprehension. Only the act of reading the books offers that possibility, or that great and solemn consolation so essential to human beings cocooned by technologies immune to human fear.

THERE'S NO PLACE LIKE HOME

DANNY MEYER

NEW YORK has arguably become the world's preeminent restaurant city. The roaring 1990s created a ripe environment for seasoned restaurateurs and neophytes alike to launch new ventures that were creative, well-funded, thoroughly researched, highly designed, and abundantly stocked with culinary talent. Augmenting that fertile set of circumstances was a rare moment in history where the world's cultural winds blew at incredible crosscurrents, depositing seeds of possibility right on to the doorstep of New York restaurateurs and chefs.

With all that irresistible culinary richness in our city, how is it, then, that I often find myself craving—almost preferring—the opportunity to dine out in at least twenty *other* cities around the world? Why is it such a challenge for me every time I'm faced with picking a restaurant in New York? I've wondered about this phenomenon for a long time. (And given my dependence on the loyalties of New York diners for my livelihood, I do hope I'm an aberration.)

It strikes me that the real reasons we visit restaurants are to satisfy three distinctively different needs: transportation, nurture, and nourishment—in that order. Great restaurants don't just do the cooking and dishes for you. They're the equivalent of a short vacation from your norm—whatever your norm may be. That's why it's called dining *out*.

I knew something was up when I once needed to select a San Francisco hotel for an overnight business stay. I picked one specifically based on its excellent dining room, only to end up dining at another restaurant later that evening—a 10-minute taxi ride away. And even though I'm fortunate to live just blocks from some of New York's very best restaurants, more often than not, I find myself overlooking those proximate venues for the opportunity to try something farther away.

And that's my problem in New York. Being the operator of five restaurants in the Big Apple has fostered a predicament where I just can't dine out in a fine restaurant and feel transported. For one thing, I'm going from work, to work. From norm to norm. Sitting down with me in a New York restaurant (especially if it is one of my own) is to see me drive myself, and usually my guests, crazy. It is fiendishly difficult for me to stop noticing and caring about all the details and things I obsess over intently throughout the day as a restaurateur. I attempt to be with my dinner guest and separate from my profession, but my mind races and rotates like a lighted ticker banner in Times Square:

How efficient and friendly was the reservation process? How swift, genuine, and warm was the welcome at the door? Does the restaurant smell good? How's the sound level? Is the music appropriate and is the volume set correctly? Are the lights set at their proper levels? Are the menus and wine list attractive and are any items "86'ed"? Are there smudge marks on the serviceware? Is the waiter someone with whom I'm going to enjoy sharing my dinner for the next few hours? (In many cases this well-meaning person knows I'm a restaurateur and will actually spend the evening auditioning for a job. Sometimes the waiter assigned to my table used to work for me in one of my restaurants. And if so, the relationship becomes further confusing. If I'm paying the tip, is he my employee for the evening even if I'm no longer his boss?)

Ah, to be transported! When I go somewhere new—particularly when I'm unknown to the restaurant—the food tastes all the better. One of my favorite pastimes is to ride the subway with my six-year-old son and go anywhere within the four non-Manhattan boroughs (plus Harlem) where I might find an ethnic hideaway. We've taken underground trips in under 45 minutes to Mexico, Venezuela, Thailand, Shanghai, Canton, Texas, North Carolina, Mississippi, Senegal, India, Egypt, Morocco, Sicily, Naples, Cuba, Korea, Japan, and France. By doing a little bit of research, it's hard to go wrong. Almost without exception, we enjoy an anthropology lesson and dine exceptionally well at the hands of someone whose pride in their native food completes the triumvirate of transportation, nurture, and nourishment.

I suspect transportation is why I first fell in love with restaurants as a student in Italy and France. There's nothing quite as deliciously satisfying as plunking down in a totally new place where people speak, cook, look, smell, dress, eat, drink, and act differently. Shopping in foreign farmer's markets or even supermarkets transports me. (This same phenomenon must hold true when shopping for nonfood items. With prices equivalent to those found in New York, why *else* would people travel to Paris to buy an Hermès scarf, or to Milan to buy a Prada purse?)

I remember how transported I felt when, as a college student in Connecticut, I'd drive down to New York for frequent weekend jaunts. The city jolted me with an electric current unlike anything I'd ever felt in Hartford, or while growing up in St. Louis. After nearly twenty-five years here, I've become inured to that buzz. I've become one of those New Yorkers and I'm finding it more and more of an elusive challenge to get the transportation I need. It's as if someone took the caffeine out of my coffee.

Often, the solution lies in my wallet, the three most utilized denizens of which are my MetroCard (every subway ride translates into a trip somewhere—at least into another neighborhood), my credit card (I need it to purchase airline tickets), and my driver's license (not just for driving, but as my only photo I.D., increasingly I need it to go almost anywhere).

But here's the most ironic thing of all: as I've

increasingly spent more time in restaurants and logged even more miles traveling and exploring places that are new, the most satisfying transportation is to return to the places I already know and—better still—to go *nowhere*. There's no trip like staying at home, thumbing through my cookbook collection, and preparing food from scratch in my own kitchen.

As my world—this world—gets more and more frenzied and fraught with uncertainty, my ultimate transportation is found in the comfort of things that are close and real. Learning a little more about much just doesn't satisfy like learning much more about a little. It's pretty easy to realize that by spending more time at home with family, friends, and with my own two hands. As James Beard used to say whenever he was asked what his favorite restaurant was, "Why, it's the one that knows me the best and loves me the most." Now that sounds a lot like home. Perhaps I'm wrong about transportation after all. It may be that nurture and nourishment are more than enough.

TILLING THE FIELDS
OF NEW YORK'S
BOOK COUNTRY

MARY POPE OSBORNE

N THE LATE 1970S, when my husband and I were first married, we lived on Bleecker Street in Greenwich Village. In those days, the Village was not such an expensive place to live. No one in our circle of friends had a "real" job. Most of us worked in restaurants or bars, moved furniture, or got occasional gigs as actors, singers, or musicians. I myself worked as a waitress and bartender at night; and during the day I tried to learn how to be a writer.

Our apartment was a sixth floor walk-up in a prewar tenement. Hardly more than 300 square feet, it had no sink in the bathroom, creaky floorboards, plaster that never stopped crumbling, clanking radiators, and a thin layer of soot over everything, all the time.

The limitations of our living quarters were manage-
able, though, because our home didn't end at the walls
of our apartment. All of New York City felt like home.

Nearly every day, no matter the season, I'd search
for a place to think, read, and write. The impulse to
leave home and "go out and play" perhaps originated
in my military childhood when I spent countless unsu-
pervised hours in the woods or on the beaches and
parade fields of the army posts where I grew up. For
me, the wonder of New York was that one could still
live like a child and no one seemed to disapprove.

In warm weather, my travels often began on our
rooftop. As the cleaning vehicles swished down the
morning streets, I'd sit with a cup of tea in a director's
chair overlooking Christopher and Bleecker and read
and write. I might get a second cup of tea and read
more and write more at a café on Sixth Avenue and
West Fourth Street called La Groceria. Then I might
venture to Washington Square Park, or to the garden
beside St. Luke's Church. If I felt like roaming really
far from home, I might spend the afternoon on the
Staten Island ferry or find a bench in Central Park.

I kept 3 x 5 cards in the pockets of my jeans at all
times. As I wandered the city, I made lists of colors and

tried to describe how light fell at different times of day. I wrote about the weather—how snow piled up on steps and sidewalks, how spring rain pelted black umbrellas moving down gray streets.

When I got home, I'd type up my scribbles on a portable typewriter in our clothes closet—which was not really a closet because there weren't any closets in that apartment. But behind a curtain that hung from the ceiling covering a rack of clothes, I searched for my voice as a writer.

Eventually, my daily travels led me into city libraries. I sat for many hours at the Jefferson Market Library and the Hudson Park Library. I discovered the Mechanic's Library in midtown. I was a regular visitor at the libraries of the Carl Jung Institute and the Museum of Natural History. I loved the reading room at the Public Library on Forty-second Street and the austere stacks of the NYU Bobst Library where a Village resident could apply for a community card that allowed him or her to work inside the library, but not check out books.

Ironically, once I discovered New York City's libraries, I became increasingly obsessed with nature. I spent hours reading books that identified trees, flowers, birds, and wild animals. I practically memorized a book called *Lost Country Life*, about farming in medieval England. I read Edwin Way Teale's and Jean Henri Fabre's books about the bizarre behavior of insects. I found that in libraries, wonderful words could be gathered and bound, like straw bundles. I made long lists of nature words, such as hollyhock, hayrick, thicket, goldenrod, may-apple. These evocative words took root and whole worlds began to sprout in my imagination. In a place with no fields or forests, I began to write stories about pigs, chickens, and cottage gardens. Admittedly, the inhabitants of my imaginary pastoral world revealed a distinct urban influence. My pigs tap-danced. My field insects had a jazz band. My chickens wore Bermuda shorts.

Once I became a published children's book author, I mined New York libraries for more treasures that led to story ideas. I read mythology, folklore, and fairy tales. For a collection of mermaid legends, I found a Japanese Sea Queen at the Jung Library and an Algonquin waterfall maid at the library of the Museum of Natural History. When I decided to write a book about American tall tale heroes, I went to the Forty-second Street Library and found the first article written about Johnny

Appleseed in a nineteenth-century *Harper's* magazine. I also read an 1848 play featuring New York tall tale hero Mose the Fireboy. When I was researching my books of historical fiction, I went to the library at the New-York Historical Society and read newspapers published at the time of Lincoln's death and on the day after Pearl Harbor.

Today I live primarily in Connecticut. But it was in New York that I learned how to carry the power of make-believe with me wherever I go. New York was stimulating to me precisely because it was so crowded and noisy and inescapable. The sound of traffic and jackhammers drove me into other worlds. In the words of seventeenth-century poet Andrew Marvell, New York urged my mind to "withdraw into its happiness." Now, the worlds I roamed in my imagination are as real to me as if I'd truly been there. In some ways, looking back, they seem *more* real. I remember my dreamscapes better than many places I've actually visited. I really feel that I've swam with mermaids and sat around campfires with Johnny Appleseed and Davy Crockett.

When I do visit New York these days my favorite places to read and scribble are the reading rooms of the

New York Society Library on Seventy-ninth Street and the atrium at the Metropolitan Museum of Art. Sitting in these places, with my books and note cards, I never know what might happen. Recently, I stumbled upon a haunted castle. I turned into a raven and flew through the night to the top of a mountain.

When we were young and lived on Bleecker Street,

anything seemed possible.

Now, more than 60 books later,

I see that it is.

ODE TO PELHAM BAY, A BRONX NEIGHBORHOOD

CYNTHIA OZICK

Old writer, bad rhymester, I count among the also-rans:

you'll find below not much that scans.

Forty years halted

from scribbling verse,

I rise exalted,

to rehearse

my town! Not your west, not your east,

not your fabled streets—legend's yeast—

that stamp their fame

with Broadway's name

in glossy magazines.

Come, come, turn away

from heavy hitters

and all that glitters!

Come north with me to Pelham Bay
and lost, forgotten scenes:
Bronx, Outer Borough, end of subway line,
vacant lots, weeds that smell like wine,
patchwork yards where lilacs droop,
a stucco house with a six-step stoop.
It's nineteen-thirty-five!
(You were not alive.)
The milkman's horse's turds attract the birds,
dandelions sprout in herds.
In summer heat the tar roads ooze,
the melting gunk sticks to your shoes.
The park is wild, unpaved, and free
and heads down meadows to the sea.
Not sea exactly, just a bay.
(City Island's across the way.)
Its ice as solid as a brick,
the bay one winter froze so thick
that we could stride from shore to shore,
sliding on a polished floor.

Topped by an Angel, shining gilt,
The Soldiers' Monument was built.
An autogyro flew

(helicopter to the likes of you)
dropping roses and carnations
to celebrate the peace of nations.
We children lifted up our arms
to catch the falling swarms,
and I remember standing on my toes
to pluck a parachuting rose.

Statuary filled the park.
Frogs croaked in the dark
in fountains carved of stone.
In moonlight, togas shone
on goddesses and sprites.
These were our delights!
An urban planner deemed them blights;
our park became his prey.
He swept the nymphs away.

Three trucks came by one night
and chose a parking site
before a concrete maze
—our stadium—to put on plays.
The first truck's ample side
slid apart to open wide.

The wonder of our age—
suddenly a stage!
First truck, Act One.
When that was done,
the second truck on cue
began Act Two.
Excitement grew,
it ran amuck:
Act Three, third truck!
We heard a shot!
It was the middle of July.
The night was hot.
(I fanned a cardboard fan.)
In that enchanted van
we all saw Lincoln die.
The three trucks rolled away.
Courtesy of WPA
Art had come to Pelham Bay.

Once a week, on rubber tires,
We knew the height of our desires.
On Friday afternoons,
in snow or in monsoons,
the Traveling Library stopped

on a corner where a yard

held some living lard.

A pig, a real live pig! It hopped

around its pen. We children gazed,

amazed, when crash! upon the grass (or mud)

two boxes landed with a thud.

We rushed them as if crazed,

fairy books in one, stories in the other.

Popular Mechanix for my brother.

But oh, the heartless rule—two per child!

Under a Sabbath light

we read and read all Friday night,

and then our books were finished.

It made us wild

to wait a week, and yet we must!

Slowly the days diminished.

Booklessly we burned

with reading lust

until the Library returned.

Pelham Bay, my Bronx, my sky!

Let no envious eye demur

if I keep you as you were,

cattails spiking high,

snake-spit on a crabgrass leaf,

A vagrant pheasant on the reef.

Yet now is now, and then was then.

Will the Traveling Library come again?

In inmost mind

I look to find

the autogyro's near-descent,

the Angel on the Monument,

the brilliant walk across the ice.

Dreaming will suffice

to swim these in our ken,

though now is now and then was then.

MICROPHONE CHECK

WILLIE PERDOMO

I HAVE READ and performed, or spit and kicked my verse to audiences in Lincoln Center, Town Hall, Central Park, and Brooklyn Bridge; crowds at conferences, coffeehouses, colleges, and cultural centers all over America, Europe, and the Caribbean have been privy to my riff sets, workshop readings, and black box testimonials. After a while, it's hard to distinguish one reading from another. The spotlights blind you and the applause deafens you. But every time a journalist or a workshop student asks where I started reading my poetry in public, my reply is always, "This place on the Lower East Side called The Nuyorican Poets Café." Not New Yorkian Café, New Rican Café, but the Nuyo-ree-can Café.

In memoir mode, I think of the first time I went to the Café. It was a goose down, skull cap, Timberland boot kind of cold in 1991. I see myself coming out of the Astor Place train station, spilling into a city pocket where everything was truly *all good*. I had a binder with freshly typed copies of the only poems I had ever written, some of which would appear in my first collection, *Where a Nickel Costs a Dime*, to be published five years later. I walk east, passing the overpriced vintage clothing stores, tattoo parlors with Lou Reed wannabe's hanging out front, and curbside booksellers. At that time I was feeding myself walks that Langston took through Harlem, the apocalyptic verses of Public Enemy, and some albums from my mother's *salsa* collection. I knew that I wanted my work to be like Romare Bearden's *The Block*, a completely interactive experience; one where you would have to be on the block or walk down the avenue to experience its life.

When I reached Third Street and Avenue B, I noticed the familiar trappings of a *barrio:* the salsa blaring out of the bodegas, the view of housing projects towering over Avenue D, and abandoned lots with cultural motifs. I felt like I was going to read poems on my block in East Harlem.

The original Nuyorican aesthetic was developed by outlaw troubadours who used poems as tools for survival; and they used Spanglish, street slang, and bomba and plena rhythms to write them. I knew this because I had discovered a copy of *Nuyorican Poetry* in a used book store in Ithaca, New York, Autumn Leaves Used Books. The progenitor of this school and co-editor of the aforementioned title, Professor Miguel Algarín, would show up at the Café later that evening. His other half, the award-winning playwright Miguel Piñero was resting in peace, having had his request to have his ashes scattered through the Lower East Side fulfilled.

I arrived at the front door and checked in with Julio, the Café's burly house manager, security guard, and source of consolation for dispirited slam poets. I told him that I was there to read some poems and that I was supposed to see "Bob," who turned out to be Bob Holman, New York City's main poetry advocate, who was hosting the slam at the Café. I noticed the audience was a bit sparse, but would get packed enough to be intimate. There was an edge, it was hip and smoky with interlude music that ranged from Ray Baretto to Miles Davis, Patti Smith to Gil-Scott Heron. It had not yet become an internationally renowned poetry venue.

that would be a success springboard for many writers, musicians, and actors. The Café was just starting the slam competitions, the "spoken word artist" label was a few years away, and Julio, the bouncer, cleared the floor after the slams to make way for the disco dancers. There were some faces from the old Sixth Street crowd like Bimbo Rivas who was standing by the bar like a general with Zeus' beard. Allen Ginsberg called the Café the most "multicultural place on the planet." It was true. I read against poets with names like Adrienne Su, Indran Amirthanayagan, and Nicole Breedlove.

I was not aware that poetry slams were like diving competitions as I heard Bob rattle off a score of 29.35 for one of the qualifying poets. I thought it was going to be just a few poets getting together and sharing their work. It was definitely a sign that hip-hop had a big influence on what was happening. It was as if I was a rapper and I was about to get into a battle. Luckily, my first mentor, Ed Randolph, had let me know that a poet is never supposed to say, "This poem is about . . ." before his delivery. I was spared the wrath of Professor Steve Cannon, the blind literary magazine publisher and Tribes Gallery owner. A few poets started prefacing their poems and Steve would yell from his designated seat at the rear of the bar, "I want to hear the poem!" The poet would laugh along with the audience and continue with his preamble and Steve would yell louder, "I want to hear a poem!" I laughed to myself and said *this place is wild*. At the Café, and through the spoken word movement, poems need no explanations. They explode into a life form of their own as soon as the words are delivered into space.

The Café has become one the most recognized poetry venues in the world. It's not odd to see lines that sometimes stretch to the pizza parlor on the corner. Poets that have stepped to the mic for the first time at the Café have gone on to make movies, write and perform on Broadway, produce records, and have disappeared into the woods to write the great epic that only twenty-seven people have read. The cafe's history has sometimes been revised, but the electricity conducted by a hot poem on a Friday night at the Café is enough to keep the projects by Avenue D lit through the graveyard shift. I've heard elitists bash the Café because you can get on its stage and read a shopping list and call yourself a poet. And I say, "Sure, almost anything goes at the Café. But sometimes that 'anything' can be better than nothing."

SAMBA

ROBERT PINSKY

The Hudson's not a river but an estuary. *Palisades Park*
Was a hit, then a jingle, or was it the other way round?

What's the difference? Or is it a difference O City of
Makers, among measures of freedom & commerce? It is

So a river because it is The Hudson River. In the same
Restaurant where Dick Powell ate with Veronica Lake,

Pacino shoots Hayden in the forehead & he falls face first
Into his spaghetti—making the place still more desirable to

Us from across the River & beyond, stunned too by live
Reindeer at Bloomie's. Donder & Blixen are caribou.

On the screen an old Eskimo with a caribou-bone needle
And thread of caribou sinew stitches together a raincoat

From strips of caribou gut. "You make use of every part
Of the caribou?"— the filmmaker's voice. The old guy

Smiles answering in Inuit while we wait for the subtitle —
"Everything but the shit!"— laughing as he keeps sewing:

Like a City answer, that profane assurance & fatalism.
A Canal herbalist might sell tincture of caribou droppings

For your cancer or your orchids. City of healers & cheaters.
Streets of sowers & killers, weavers & reapers. In front of

"Goan Foods" the vender of girly lighters & bargain
CDs is dickering with his customer. They were born on

Different continents & the CD is not shit, it is the many-
Rooted music of the great Brazilian, Caetano Veloso.

SEPTEMBER IN NEW YORK, PUBLIC & ELEMENTARY

MARIE PONSOT

As if speech could have
sparks leaping in it (like

    the way the new lover says, "Welcome home, love,"

    or the new softball captain says, "Let's go, gang")

once upon a time she

    with her soft fast glance

    collecting them said,

    "Good morning, class,"

and all her seated uplooking

    second-graders quickly said,

    "Good morning, Miss McKnight,"

    ready, hearts hammering,

    her gang, her lovers, her class.

SCHOOL LUNCH

RUTH REICHL

THE FORSYTHIA BLOOMED earlier on West
Eleventh Street than anywhere else in the city.
You could see it poking up through the snow as you
turned off Sixth Avenue, and feel the sun beating down,
harder here. People stood on the sidewalk staring at the
flowers, and when they looked up at the Rhinelander
Gardens, graceful homes with languid porches wrapped
in wrought iron, they always heard soft laughter. Suddenly they'd smell shrimp and chiles, lime and vanilla,
and start dreaming of gumbo and coconut cream pie.

Then the city tore down The Gardens and put an
ugly public school in its place. In the fall of 1955 Mrs.
Pinski told her fifth-grade class to pack up their
belongings and say good-bye to the old school. It was

time to move around the corner to the new one. We marched out clutching our pencil boxes and our notebooks chanting "Buffalo Bill's defunct" in our loudest voices as we passed Patchen Place, just in case e.e. cummings, who lived there, might be listening. We were still chanting as we walked up Sixth Avenue. And then we turned the corner and felt the cold and knew that the warm weather had gone with the Rhinelander Gardens. There were no flowers, no gumbo, no coconut. We stared glumly at the new school.

The old P.S. 41 was a ramshackle place, a pile of crumbling bricks built before the Civil War. It lacked a gym, a playground, and a lunchroom. We didn't care. We were Village kids. We glared at the playground they had given us, a dark cement triangle that lurked outside, looking menacing and cold. We hated it. And then we went through the doors and walked down the halls, sniffing plaster and fresh paint. As we approached the sparkling new cafeteria we came to a horrified halt. We looked at all those chairs and tables, instantly understanding what they meant: The end of the feast.

In normal schools the children went to cafeterias where they were served slices of gray meat, lumpy mashed potatoes, and canned string beans. At P.S. 41 we went home for lunch. Going to my house was no thrill: Mom was a terrible cook and her lunches were embarrassing reruns of the horrid dinner we'd eaten the night before. But the mothers took turns feeding us, sending us off in little groups to savor an international banquet.

The best days were when we went home with Cristina, who lived above her parents' restaurant on Christopher Street. You could smell the garlic as soon as you opened the door. For a New York kid in the fifties it was a strange and wonderful scent, and we all wanted to be her friend. Cristina's mother urged us to eat in a lilting Sicilian accent, offering seconds and thirds of homemade pizza, which none of us had ever seen before. The square slices were soft and yeasty, piled high with fresh tomatoes and melted cheese that amazed us with its power to stretch into delicious long strands. She asked if we had ever tried lasagna (no), or canneloni (definitely not) and shook her head sadly at our answers. Each time we showed up she tried to surprise us with something new. Once it was cactus pears, the color beneath the green skin so rich and vibrant that I fell in love before I even tasted the sweet, fragrant flesh. And if we were very lucky, we'd hear the whisk hitting her copper bowl and know that she was making zabaglione, soft clouds that floated into your mouth and vanished instantly, like magic.

We had to take our shoes off at the door of Rodney Murai's spare and lovely house. Inside, the table was on the floor; sitting barefoot and crosslegged made every meal seem so much like something out of *Mary Poppins* that we unprotestingly ate rice cakes wrapped in shiny black paper tasting of the sea. It would be thirty years until I learned that I had been eating seaweed, but at the time it was as unfamiliar as the tofu his mother served, tiny bites of cool white cubes. It was creamy and cold in the mouth, like some startlingly unsweetened ice cream, and I loved it almost as much as the shards of ginger, with their sharply piquant flavor, scattered across the top.

Nancy Henenfeld's mother worked, which gave lunch at her house a decidedly exotic quality. When we rang the bell gruff Nellie, the housekeeper, came to the door. From the hissing and spitting in the kitchen we could tell that she was cooking fried chicken which burned our mouths when we bit into the crisp, juicy drumsticks. But nobody's mom made fried chicken (the grease!), and we stuffed ourselves until our throats were on fire and Nellie had to hand us tall cold glasses of lemonade to quench the flames. Afterward there were the softest biscuits, slathered with butter and jam, which fell into rich crumbs each time you took a bite. I was a little scared of Nellie, but that only made the food taste better.

Lunch at Peter Taber's house was also an adventure. His father was a journalist who had been gone for months on some mysterious assignment. His mother said he was up in the mountains with Fidel Castro. When we asked what it was like over there in Cuba she served us rice and beans with a fried egg on top, so we could taste the island. I liked it so much that I longed to go there—even before she told us about the crisp pork that they cooked over coals up in the mountains, or the fish she said came leaping from the sea down by the shore.

And then there were the days we went to lunch at my best friend Jeanie's house. Her mother made perfectly respectable sandwiches, pale squares of cream cheese on white bread. But often her grandmother was there when we arrived, unpacking pickles from Gus', smoked fish from Russ and Daughters, and knishes from Yonah Shimmel. On the best days there was also borscht, which she slathered with sour cream so that it looked like a tropical sunset in a bowl. Fifteen years later, when I wrote my cookbook, it was the first recipe I requested.

By then it was too late to get recipes from any of the other families. Cristina moved to Long Island when we were in sixth grade, and Nellie went back south when Nancy outgrew babysitters. I lost track of the boys during high school. So I scoured the city streets, searching for remembered flavors, combing Little Italy, the Lower East Side, Chinatown, and Spanish Harlem, begging the shopkeepers for recipes.

"Where did you learn all these foreign dishes?" asked my editor when I handed in the manuscript. "What cooking school did you attend?"

"I never went to cooking school," I said.

There was a short, embarrassed silence. My editor was a nice woman—she was even letting me call my cookbook *Mmmmm*—and I wanted very much to give her an acceptable answer. And then, all at once, it came to me.

"Actually," I heard myself say, "I did study world cuisine. It was at P.S. 41 and the class was called school lunch."

NUEVA YO

ESMERALDA SANTIAGO

I N   P U E R T O   R I C O in the 1950s and 1960s when we said "New York," we meant the United States. Actually, we didn't say New York. We translated it to *Nueva Yol*, or *los nuevayores*.

To my ears, *los nuevayores* sounded as if those who had gone there came back as new people, suggested by the Spanish for new (*nueva*) in the feminine, and I (*yo*), pluralized into yores, grammatically incorrect but suggestive of a change that was not necessarily an improvement. I thought that people who had lived in New York became more than one I, and were now at least two separate individuals, the Puerto Rican and the North American. Little did I know how close I was to the truth. Those of us who come to *los nuevayores* do become different people, a phenomenon we describe as schizophrenia because of the dual personas we develop to cope with two cultures, two languages, conflicting values and contradictory expectations.

Except for Tío Lalo, who returned to San Juan, my mother's uncles settled in *Nueva Yol* after serving in World War II. They lured their sisters to work in the factories and hotels of the City. Soon, letters with money, packages with pretty dresses for the girls and jeans for the boys arrived regularly from relatives known to us only by their addresses or fuzzy black-and-white snapshots, their faces shadowed by brimmed hats.

"A package from Tía Chía!" I called when her neatly wrapped parcels arrived at our door.

"Gifts from Titi Ana!" my sister Delsa yelled when a box was dropped off by our equally excited mailman.

"Ay, que bueno!" Mami exclaimed, caressing an envelope from her mother, whom we called Tata, in which she might find a money order that had reached her when most needed.

To Mami, *Nueva Yol* represented abundance, opportunity, a warm and loving family. To us children it was the land of Cool Things. The packages that arrived crushed or banged up from the trip across the Atlantic held won-

ders like no one else in our barrio had seen. For Hector, a
real Hopalong Cassidy holster with guns that fired caps
dotted on a paper ribbon. For Edna, a monkey that
shrieked and clapped tiny cymbals when she wound the
key on his back. Tata sent me a bright yellow purse that
clicked closed when I slid the hasp into the loop. I had
nothing to put inside it, and was not the sort of girl who
carried a purse, but I loved owning something so pretty.

The gifts and money were exciting, but just as often
Airmail envelopes with red and blue edges arrived from
Nueva Yol with bad news. Uncle Chico, who worked as
a cook in a hotel, slipped on a lettuce leaf and broke his
leg. He was out of work for months, and had to move in
with Tía Chía. Tata was laid-off from the girdle factory,
which is why there was no check in her Christmas letter, and her presents to us girls were clothes already
worn by Titi Ana's daughters. The boys got handker-
chiefs. A cousin had chicken pox and another cousin
who was pregnant caught it and miscarried her baby. A
fire forced Uncle Pipo, his wife, and three children into
a Red Cross shelter before Cousin Margot located them
and brought them to her one room apartment. The
story of our relatives in *Nueva Yol* was a series of
calamities tempered by short-lived celebrations for a

new job, a new apartment or by the hope that next week, next month, next year, things would be better.

It was inevitable that we, too, would go to *Nueva Yol*. After fourteen years together, Mami and Papi did not get along. Papi's income as a carpenter and mason wasn't enough for a family of two adults and seven children. He both appreciated and resented the money and gifts that Mami's relatives sent. While they lightened his burden, they also proved that he was incapable of meeting his obligation as husband and father. He disappeared, sometimes for weeks. His absences hinted at another life that didn't include us.

Mami must have been planning the trip for a long time, but I didn't know we were leaving Puerto Rico until a few days before we landed in *Nueva Yol*. We came to Brooklyn to Wilinsber, a neighborhood near Booswi. When I learned enough English, I understood that *Nueva Yol* was, like Puerto Rico, a series of barrios with distinctive names and character. From Williamsburg, we would soon move to Bushwick, where Mami's relatives lived. From there, we went to Is New Yol (East New York) and later, Befor Styvess (Bedford Stuyvesant). We became Brooklyn Puerto Ricans, and settled in our neighborhoods in our borough, seldom venturing to other Puerto Rican enclaves in the Bronx, Loisaida (Lower East Side) or El Barrio.

In Puerto Rico, we had never lived higher than a ground floor, and it took me a while to get used to the verticalness of *los nuevayores*. I climbed the stairs of those first apartment buildings with trepidation, peeking over the banisters as the ground dropped beneath my shoes, afraid to lean over too far and hurtle toward the hard tiled floors.

Until we arrived here, New York had been the picture postcard of a jagged horizon of skyscrapers. Once I was inside those tall buildings, *Nueva Yol* became a steep climb to a succession of landings leading to long, dim hallways with doors on either side from which emanated familiar smells and sounds. Sofrito sputtered in an unseen kitchen that was probably in the same location as ours, two floors up. My favorite singer, Bobby Capó, crooned a cha-cha-cha inside another apartment. The doors lining the hallways opened only if the people behind them knew me, or trusted me, or if they wanted to drag me into a dark apartment and commit unspeakable cruelty on an innocent girl.

Fear and shame were the dominant emotions of those

first few years in *los nuevayores*. Chief among my worries was to get home safely from school, or the store, or wherever I happened to be. Those doors lining those dim halls were locked and bolted for a reason. The world beyond our threshold was a cruel and violent place, in which I could be lost, physically and psychologically. Each one of the closed doors on my floor, in my building, on the block, the neighborhood, the City, represented another world. Walking through one of them required a willingness to be judged, evaluated, and usually, found lacking.

Los nuevayores, for all its promise and excitement, was also the place where people like me—foreign, dark skinned, poor—were expected not only to fail at whatever we attempted, but to take whole neighborhoods with us as we fell further from "mainstream," which meant Caucasian middle class society. The proof was all around me. It lurked in the suspicious eyes of the shopkeeper who didn't live in my barrio but took my money, then wiped his hands on his stained apron. Teachers steered even the brightest of us to vocational schools because they saw no hope that we would succeed in college. Taxi drivers refused to deliver us to our address because *they* were afraid of the neighborhood. Newspapers only reported stories about Puerto Ricans if the more frustrated of us had committed a crime. Television shows were a sea of white faces and no one in them ever ventured into Is New Yol, Booswi or Befor Styvess. The villain that threatened their compact neighborhoods always had the features of someone I knew.

The round hills and curved paths of the Puerto Rican countryside I had known retreated to my dreams. Reality was the austere straightness of New York City blocks tightly packed with identical two-dimensional buildings. The soft vowels and trilling r's of Spanish offered me comfort within our apartment and inside my head, while the rest of the world barked its guttural Anglo-Saxon.

"New York, New York, is a wonderful town," sang Gene Kelly and Frank Sinatra. "I want to live in America," sang Rita Moreno and the Sharks on the rooftops of *West Side Story*. I asked myself, where are the poor people in that New York? Where are the people who don't speak English, the ones who can't afford a night on the town? I did not know a single gang member who spent his time singing on the roof. If they were up there, it was because they had just shoved someone over the edge. Where are the factory workers, I wondered, where are the busboys, the maids, the men who pushed covered racks of designer clothes in the garment center? Did they all live only in my neighborhood, where Hollywood wouldn't venture?

Perhaps I thought too much, analyzed too much, worried too much. Those first years in *Nueva Yol* taught me that the United States was not as welcoming as the image of the Statue of Liberty in New York Harbor would have us believe. It meant to draw us in, I thought, then spit us out, defeated and worse off than when we arrived. When we came here we brought nothing more than hope and optimism; *Nueva Yol* meant to squeeze that hope and optimism out of us.

One day, Mami brought me to the welfare office, to interpret her desperation, even though my English was only slightly better than hers. In the despair of a roomful of women like her, begging for their future, I saw mine. Old or young, each of those women was once a girl with dreams and ambitions eroded by hardship. Help me, they asked when they heard me interpret for Mami. Help me, they wanted me to say on their behalf to the harried, short-tempered social workers. Mami and I were in that office for hours after our case was heard as I translated for other women, some of them in greater need of help than we were.

When we walked out of the welfare office, we were in another of the long hallways lined with doors that defined *los nuevayores* for me. Rather than go past them as quickly as I could, I took a deep breath, opened each door, and looked in at the reception counter of a dental practice, at the production room of an advertising company, at the file cabinets lining the walls of an insurance agency, at the expectant waiting room of an obstetrician. Not one dark face greeted me, not like in the welfare office where almost every supplicant was brown. When I was asked with veiled contempt, or sometimes fear, whether I could be "helped," I said "No, just looking," and closed the door firmly behind me. With that gesture, I refused to be intimidated by New York. From then on, I would barge in, welcome or not, where I was not wanted.

A long, empty hallway lined with doors has haunted my dreams since I arrived at Idlewild Airport on a wet, shimmering night in August 1961. It is the tunnel-like intensity of that long hallway scored with thresholds that comes to mind whenever a challenge presents itself, a decision has to be made, a step has to be taken that has not been taken before. *Los nuevayores* has made me brave, and it has created the curious hybrid that is the Puerto Rican New Yorker, bound to one culture while living in another. A nueva yo.

OCTOBER 12, 2002

DENNIS SMITH

I T F E E L S S O R E C E N T, so planted near the surface of the psyche, that it is hard to acknowledge
that almost four hundred days have passed. The city's
skyscrapers seem to shake as I study them through the
sheets of early morning rain. Perhaps they are nervous
and uncertain like I am, like any one of us in the fire
service might be today. The day of ceremony and
memory has arrived. It is an important day.

We are in bumper-grating traffic on Seventh Avenue. I think of the numerous times I have been on this
same road, bumping south on Fashion Avenue, heading
for Madison Square Garden, tickets in hand for basket-
ball or hockey games, for circuses or rodeos, ice spectac-
ulars or bagpipe competitions. But, the gray pallor of

the wet city redounds on any sense of joy that normally comes with visiting the Garden. This is not a normal day with normal expectations, but a day of remembering the worst day in our history. I can feel the gravity of purpose with every drop of rain and every gust of wind.

"It won't be easy getting to Thirty-fourth Street," the cab driver says.

The blasts and screeches of the car horns are as annoying as the stalled traffic.

"Get as close as you can," I answer, "and I'll walk."

It is a Saturday. There are no racks of designer clothes being pushed by truckers along the side streets of the garment center, and the weather has swept the sidewalks of the usual end of summer midtown hordes. But the Avenue is jammed with cars and cabs, and there are limousines seen in every direction—the Hollywood stretch types, white and as long as the front of a movie marquee, and the smaller ones, black and conservative. The limos are lined as far as I can see down the Avenue, one for every family, three hundred and fifty-six in all.

I think of the firefighters, more than fifty thousand of them from every state in the union and some from Europe, many mustering at the intersection of Eighth Avenue and Twenty-third Street, just four blocks west from where twelve firefighters fell through a floor and into the fire in 1966—until now the worst disaster in New York's firefighting history. The rest are huddled at Fourteenth Street, waiting to be marched through the wind and the rain. An honor band of bagpipers from fire departments throughout the country will follow the lead of the Emerald Society pipers of FDNY. Behind them will be a contingent of American flag bearers, 356 flags borne by firefighters from across the land. They have traveled to stand straight, rain or shine, to carry an American flag that will represent a valorous life given in the line of duty. Each flag bearer knows the name of the person the flag honors—three hundred and forty-three active firefighters, three retired firefighters, and one member of the Fire Patrol (the insurance under-writers' salvage corps) who died that fateful day of September 11, 2001, and nine firefighters who have died in the line of duty in the previous months of 2001, or in the eleven months since. Three hundred and fifty-six flag bearers—each one thinking of a hero's name as the rain soaks through the wool of his or her uniform.

The image brings me back to Boston where I attended the funerals of eight firefighters who died at the Vendome Building fire in 1972, and the rain that fell on that sad day. Thousands of firefighters were quickly passed a clear plastic raincoat and a pair of white gloves, donated by an unnamed citizen to keep them a little dry, and to present a sense of white gloved uniformity. On this day, though, no one has thought of providing raincoats, and the chill of the constant curtain of rain and wind is taken as a badge of what will be a proud memory, for no inconvenience can compare to the loss that moves us today.

The cab gets to Thirty-third Street, and I dash to dry safety beneath the entryway of the Garden. There is a bobbing wave of men and women in blue uniforms, and I fall naturally into its movement, exchanging greetings with the many I know, and nodding "How ya doing?" to those I don't.

"Hey Dennis," one calls to me, "I haven't seen you since the 149th Street job, on that roof, remember, with Buddy Croce, when it caved."

"I just got a letter from Buddy," I answer. "He's in Virginia, living the good life."

There is something to remember about every fire, I think, and when this man and I and Buddy were together in the 1970s we responded from fire to fire, sometimes never getting back to the firehouse for dinner.

There were so many fires, and so many memories. I don't remember the fire he cites, but I suppose no one died and no one was hospitalized, for I never forget those fires.

I make my way through the maze of corridors to my gate, and then my section, and then my row. Another man calls my name. It sounds like Dan Potter who comes from my old firehouse on Intervale Avenue. He was caught by the collapse of the South Building, and then again by the collapse of the North Building, as he sought to find his wife who was on the eighty-first floor of the North Tower, just a hundred feet from the plane as it hit. He injured enough bones in his body from the fall of those buildings that the department would not let him back to full duty.

But it's not Dan whom I met last week in Washington, D.C., at the National Day of Mourning for Firefighters.

"How's retirement, Dan?" I asked.

"Okay. I'm teaching rescue procedures to the volunteer firefighters on Long Island." It is reassuring that Dan has found a way to keep something of a career that was cut short by the fall of the Twin Towers. So many lives have been lost, and so many lives have been changed so thoroughly.

This firefighter before me is a retired union president,

and I exchange with him the union's thumbs up. I look around, thinking that Dan must be here as well, some-place. No one vied for the good seats at this gathering.

The Garden has a dull, echoless sound as I move around it. As the 2,500 firefighters and families arrive, this quiet sound slowly changes to chatter, like in a lobby at a musical's intermission. The firefighters are not mourning, for they have already been through a few hundred funerals and memorial services. They have held the widows by the elbows and the children by the hands, and they have left tears on the backs of pews. They seem positive and resolute, but not sad. This is a day to pay homage to our history, to show the families of our heroes that the heroism for which they have so dearly paid will never be forgotten.

Looking across the Garden's main floor I can see many friends. Joe Pfeifer who lost his brother Kevin is here, and Jim Boyle who lost his son Michael, and Lee Ielpi who lost his son Jonathan. And hundreds of oth-ers, each family joined by a department escort who will present the honors.

Rimming the ceiling are oil portraits of the fallen firefighters by Peter Max. Below them the stage is set in blue, centered by an inscribed bronze plaque. There is a wreath of 356 red and white roses set between two groups of sitting officials. On the left are the 17 uniformed fire chiefs, the power and intelligence of the department, and on the right there are 17 civilian dignitaries. No one is introduced, for this day is not about dignitaries. The plaque symbolizes all the plaques that will today be dedicated in the firehouses throughout the city, and this one bears the name of the first recorded loss of the World Trade Center, Father Mychal Judge.

The city's Fire Chief, Frank Cruthers, arrives at the podium, and the crowd comes immediately to silence as anticipation turns to expectation. The Chief speaks of Athens, how we all defend our civilization, and how duty is determined by character.

A gospel choir sings of the homeless, and we are reminded of a larger world of suffering. Harold Schaitberger, the president of the International Firefighters' Union, speaks of General McArthur, the poetry of dedication, and workers in arms. Former Mayor Giuliani speaks of lost leaders, of Bill Feehan, Ray Downey, and Father Judge. On the television screens above we can see the 50,000 firefighters, the pipes and the flags waving, marching briskly through the rain.

Mayor Bloomberg speaks so certainly of preparedness and future and change, the change that we must all understand is on the horizon. We are left with the thought of a new world order, and then Fire Commissioner Nick Scoppetta speaks of the tradition of firefighting.

A Battalion Chief begins to call the roll of honor, and a huge photo of each firefighter appears on the Garden screens. In the background, four horns play a slow fanfare, and it reminds me of the music of royalty. The names are heard, recognized, and remembered, each one, for what they did and what they gave, 356 strong. It takes nearly forty minutes, a pause after each name for remembrance. Never before had so many made an active on-the-scene choice to so forthrightly risk their lives and the futures of their families and friends. They knew the danger, and yet they went in, and climbed the stairs to reach those thousands of fellow human beings who needed them.

A string quartet plays "The Wearin' O' the Green" in a dirge tempo, and as the music ends, the names end. The Battalion Chief calls for the 356 department escorts to rise, and to present the satin-lined box of medals to the families. I see Joe Pfeifer present the mahogany box to his parents. The box is open and holds four medals of Honor. I can see the Tiffany medal in 22k vermeil, The Medal of Valor, struck especially for those who perished in the line of duty on September 11, 2001. And for all the fallen firefighters there are the department's Medal of Supreme Sacrifice, the Uniformed Firefighter's Association's and the International Association of Fire Fighter's medals of honor. Mr. and Mrs. Pfeifer take the box in their four hands, and I wonder what it is they are thinking, just as I look about the Garden and wonder what the thoughts of the other 355 families are? Most of the families are young. There are so many children, and so many tears.

A spontaneous burst of applause begins. It is loud and forceful, and it has the energy of 25,000 people, men, women, and children. This force lingers for a while, and then undulates. Suddenly, as if everyone in Madison Square Garden has come to realize that this applause has a meaning that goes much beyond mere applause, that it is a voice of despair and yearning and anguish, the Garden erupts into a wild cheer. People are yelling at the top of their lungs, and it is sustained, on and on, until it diminishes by just a decibel or two. And then the clapping rises again, and the yelling, and it begins to be supported by a rising whistling. The whistling grows and grows like a brush stroke around the arena, and it is loud and shrill and sustained, like the whistle of a huge steam engine, forcing the sound through the ears and the mind and the body. I can feel the vibrations rushing through my body, and I suddenly feel so connected to every person around me as each claps and whistles and yells, a manifestation now of something bigger than appreciation and honor, this acclamation has become an act of love and pride. It continues through the first minute and then the second. I can tell it will not end, not until these firefighters release the 397 days of pain and grief and anger they have internalized, the profound sorrow they carry within themselves every waking moment and most of their angst-filled nights.

The roar continues on and on for four minutes, and then for five. The Battalion Chief holds his hands up momentarily, but the crowd cheers louder in response. Mayor Bloomberg moves to the front of the stage, and I feel for him. His natural inclination is to take charge, to focus and direct the energy of others, but here in this din he reconsiders, and steps back. Six minutes. The whistling begins again, sharply. It goes up and down, musical to shrill, louder and louder. Eight minutes. I can feel the blood rushing through the veins of my neck as I continue the clapping, and I can sense a joy in this room among the firefighters as they realize that they are letting these families know how much their fallen loved ones were loved by all, that the love will continue and be sustained, and that this moment will carry our children forward proudly in their remembrance. This is a moment of recognizing the magnificence of lives well lived, of celebrating the heroism that has grown from the pureness of heart.

At nine minutes the applause ebbs slowly and then, satisfied, accepts an end. Madison Square Garden is again silent, and the Memorial Celebration is over.

On the way out I meet Charlie McCarthy, a man I worked with for many years in a South Bronx firehouse. He is now a retired Lieutenant, and in the midst of the throng in the section corridor of the Garden, he presents his son. I can hear the pride in his voice, as he says, "Say hello to Jim."

Jim McCarthy is wearing the uniform of a New York firefighter, and to see these two men together brings me to understand why the New York Fire Department will transcend this mortal injury it has suffered, and flourish in good deeds long into the future.

ABOUT A MOMENT

R.L. STINE

THIS IS ABOUT a mystery that probably wasn't a mystery after all. And about a longing for something that could never happen—*or could it?*

It's a story about New York—past and present—but as with many of my stories, it begins in Ohio, where I grew up. For a kid in a small, quiet, endlessly typical suburb of Columbus, New York City seemed as far away as the planet Mars.

A timid, shy, not-terribly sociable kid, I spent most of my time in my room in front of the radio. I had a big, powerful Zenith—black and silver, with a round speaker as big as my head, and a dial that glowed like yellow moonlight.

And when the moon was right, and the wind blew

west, and the clouds parted, I could pull in New York radio. My hand on the knob, carefully tuning, carefully moving through the static of local stations, I could beam in the voices of New York . . . Barry Gray, Long John Nebel, Frankie Crocker, Symphony Sid, Alan Freed, Bob & Ray, Jean Shepherd . . .

The signal faded, then disappeared, then slowly returned, and I listened with my ear pressed against the speaker. I knew the voices were calling to me, pulling me the way I carefully pulled in the distant signals . . . calling me to New York.

I couldn't resist. After college, I moved to New York and wandered the streets with such wide-eyed excitement and delight, gazing at the buildings, the people, the crowds, like an explorer in Oz.

But forget all that. This is not what I'm writing about—because just about everyone in New York is from Ohio, and just about everyone from Ohio has written about how amazed and delighted they were to be here.

My real romance with New York—and the longing that came with it—began with a book you've probably read. I'm talking about *Time and Again* by Jack Finney. Finney lived in California, but he wrote what *has* to be the most romantic book about New York City ever written.

Time and Again is about an advertising guy named Si Morley. A top-secret government agency selects Si for a time-travel experiment. He is sent back to New York of the 1880s, at first, only to observe; then his mission grows more dangerous.

How does Si slide back in time? By occupying an apartment in The Dakota, the West Side apartment building built in 1882. Si wears clothing from the 1880s. Everything in the apartment is from the period, including the newspapers Si reads. Si lives in the apartment, surrounded by details of the 1880s, wishing himself back in time, wishing . . . wishing.

And on one snowy night, he peers out of his apartment window and begins to tremble, his heart pounding—because through the falling snowflakes, he can see the glow of light from the windows of the Museum of Natural History. *No other buildings to block the museum!*

He has done it! He knows he has gone back. The Dakota and the Museum (opened in 1869) are the only two large buildings on the West Side!

Si wanders the streets of 1880s New York like an

Ohioan in the city for the first time. The *clip clop* of horses' hooves, the rattle of milk bottles, the sharp smell of manure on the crowded, cobbled streets, long-skirted, bustled women shopping the Ladies Mile, fur-coated men in bowler hats and boots, the rumble of the Third Avenue El, the buildings long lost and long forgotten— Si sees it all with wonder and amazement—and love.

Finney's time-travel book is fascinating, wonderfully detailed, and exciting. But more important than the plot is the author's *longing*.

As you read the book, you realize that Finney would give anything—*anything!*—to go back to the nineteenth century for just a *minute*. To breathe that different air, to hear what it *sounded* like, the voices, the laughter, to see the faces, so different, all so different. *Anything* for just one minute back there.

I read other books by Finney because they all had the same theme. They all were about going back in time. They all revealed the same longing.

And now, I had it, too. I took long walks around Madison Square and Gramercy Park, where much of *Time and Again* took place. I gazed at the townhouses and tried to imagine myself back in time.

I found a photo book called *Lost New York* by

Nathan Silver. I spent hours studying the wonderful buildings torn down long ago by an impatient city . . . the old Pennsylvania Station, the Hippodrome, the Crystal Palace, grand theaters and meeting halls.

My wife, Jane, and I lived two blocks from The Dakota. I thought about the Finney book every time I passed it. And I remembered the 1880s photograph of the ice-skaters in Central Park, so over-dressed, skating in front of The Dakota, the only building in sight.

One snowy day, we walked through the park and came out at The Dakota. The snow was above our ankles and still falling—a beautiful blizzard, with drifts up to our waists. "A real 1880s blizzard," I said, gazing up at the gabled roof of The Dakota, blanketed with snow.

That night, sparkling flakes still coming down, the city stood so silent, the quiet you hear only when the snow is still fresh, parked cars buried in white, the streets so empty.

It was after two in the morning. My wife and I were in bed. We had the window cracked, shades up high to watch the snow.

I sat up when I heard a sound. A soft *clip clop* out on the street.

Jane heard it too. We listened together.

Clip clop . . . clip clop . . .

It's happened! I thought. We've gone back!

I pictured the horse, the shiny, black carriage, the couple inside in their heavy furs.

Clip clop . . . clip clop . . .

I'd wished for this for so long. I jumped out of bed. I started to the window.

But Jane called me back. "Don't look," she said. "Don't look. You'll spoil it."

Clip clop . . . Clip clop. Under our window, then softer as it moved away.

I closed my eyes. I didn't move. I didn't look out.

Then, silence.

I know. I know. It was just a moment. This whole piece is about that moment. But when you have such an impossible longing, a moment can be amazing.

WHY ELECTRICMAN
LIVES IN NEW YORK

PETER STRAUB

TWO WEEKS AFTER his fortieth birthday, Electricman still feels cheerful on the surface, dark and edgy underneath. Things seem to be going all right in both halves of his odd life, but he knows that "seem" is the only accurate verb for that sentence: if things really were all right, he would not experience these odd waves of panic and despair that boil up, unpredictably, from some hidden source felt to be more or less infinite. He knows of course that he is undergoing a mid-life crisis, a common, if not ritual, passage for men of his age. Upon entering their fifth decade, males, at least American males, tend go into mourning for what is suddenly perceived as their (cruelly) vanished youth and exhibit their (largely unconscious) grief by reverting to the patterns of adolescence: increased indulgence in drugs and alcohol, and frantic skirt-chasing. Many of the afflicted neglect their jobs and suffer the shock of abrupt unemployment.

Electricman has not yet reached this pass, in either half of his life. As Arthur Groom, he continues to fulfill, however grudgingly, his duties as author of "Don't Ask Arthur," an advice column published in an alternative weekly located in the East Village and syndicated in hundreds of journals throughout the country. That he can produce his advice column from his apartment on West End Avenue greatly facilitates that side of his life in which he is obliged to shuck his clothing, slip into a hooded, skintight outfit of black Spandex emblazoned front and back with a yellow lightning-bolt, dive into the nearest electrical outlet, fly through an immense night work of wires to pop out of a wall or a transformer convenient to a crime scene, and make hay with the perps, thereby rescuing the grateful victim. The obligation to become Electricman descended upon Arthur at the age of nineteen, when, during a rain-drenched family picnic on the outskirts of his home town of Ladysmith, Wisconsin, he wandered disaffected beneath a giant oak to guzzle Gatorade he had previously spiked with Daddy Groom's Smirnoff Platinum. A lightning bolt made smoke dribble from his ears and turned his eyes buttercup yellow. When taken home, he slept for three days straight and on the fourth day discovered, neatly folded beneath his pillow, the Spandex cat-suit he has worn ever since.

"Don't Ask Arthur," frankly, has become a bore. Once, getting paid for telling young men that their girlfriends sounded much too good to abandon and young women that their boyfriends sounded like manipulative creeps had satisfied something within Arthur, perhaps the same desire for order expressed more physically in his Electricman work. Whupping the malefactors and accepting the embraces of rescued damozels could never really lose its appeal, but of late it has become tediously repetitive, almost as much so as his column. When information of a crime in progress leaks from a nearby electrical outlet and awakens his Electricman-senses, he sighs, "Oh, hell, not again—mug, mug, mug, but at least it's better than advising Larchmont Tiffany to dump two-timing Scarsdale Harry."

In his unhappiness, Electricman has taken to wearing his superhero outfit throughout most of the day, even when he goes over to Broadway to buy a salami-and-swiss on a Kaiser roll, or to wander through a museum. It makes him feel better, it bucks him up—besides that, girls, even those who loiter in the galleries of the Metropolitan Museum of Art, like a man in uniform.

"So you can sort of pick the crimes you want to foil?" asks Janet Hale, a very pretty example of the sort of young woman to be found loitering in the Met's galleries. She and Electricman are having tea in the lobby of the Carlyle Hotel, a place where Electricman can relax, uninterrupted by autograph-seekers.

"Oh, for sure," says Electricman. "Otherwise, my life would be a nightmare. You have no idea what comes down through the wires. Hour after hour, day by day. Rapes, burglaries, hold-ups, arson. Assaults with intent. Jury tampering. Mail fraud. Coupon forgery. It never stops, not for a second."

Now Janet Hale looks stricken by the sheer quantity of wickedness going on in New York. "Maybe you should think about moving somewhere smaller. You'd still be able to fight crime, there just wouldn't be so *much* of it."

Electricman sips his Darjeeling tea and appears to consider her suggestion. "Just out of curiosity, what do you like to read?"

"Lots of stuff, I guess." She glances up at the ceiling. "Don DeLillo and Donald Westlake. I read John Ashbery and Ann Lauterbach and Louise Glück. Umm, who else? Well . . . Joyce Carol Oates, Henry James, Raymond Chandler, Charles Dickens, George Pelecanos, Fernando Pessoa, Iris Murdoch . . . ."

"If you don't mind my asking, where are you from?" he asks her.

"Grand Rapids. Michigan. I moved here five years ago, right after I graduated from Ann Arbor."

"Because you had to live here. Didn't you feel that? I do. I think I could only find you, or someone like you, here in New York."

"Ah," says pretty Janet Hale.

"Here's something else. Last week, I went out on two different nights, to two different clubs. Thursday, I went to this place called Smoke, a little jazz club on 106th and Broadway. In Smoke, people don't give a damn if you're a superhero, they're too hip. It might be the best jazz club in New York. I heard a tenor player named Eric Alexander. He has a big, fat sound and great technique—he knows every single thing you can do with a tenor saxophone, and he always makes beautiful, exciting music. It's like listening to a young Sonny Stitt, or a young Dexter Gordon. Then on Saturday night, I went down to the Mercury Lounge, on Houston. The people there thought I was wearing a costume, so they didn't give a damn, either. I went to hear Future Bible Heroes, whose leader is an amazing genius named Stephin Merritt. It's like chamber pop, or something—exquisite songs with weird, quirky rhymes and gorgeous melodies."

"I begin to see the point," says Janet. "Actually, I'm crazy about Eric Alexander and Stephin Merrit, too. But right now, I'm getting into Low, the Tiger Lillies, and that trumpet player, Dave Douglas. Do you know him?"

"Not yet," Electricman says. "But I will, I promise you. Would you do me a favor?"

"What?"

"I'd like you to call me Arthur," he says. "I'm starting to feel a little more integrated than I have been lately. " He signaled to a waiter. "How about walking over to the Frick? It isn't far, and we could look at the Bellini St. Francis."

"And that Rembrandt self-portrait," Janet says, wonderfully.

"You know," Electricman says, "I really am beginning to feel much better."

GAINED IN TRANSLATION

DONALD E. WESTLAKE

I LOVED THE END of the Cold War, and the other easings of tension around the globe, but purely for selfish commercial reasons. Every time a society lightens up in some part of the world, and a movement toward democracy takes place, they start publishing American novels, and sometimes some of them are mine. (I never thought I'd be taking money out of China.)

This is true even though much of what I write is comic, and everybody knows you can't translate comedy. Nevertheless, they try, and who knows how many poor ink-stained wretches I've driven to hard drink and worse as a result. I know I've received more than one photo over the years of a translator holding a gun to his head.

In a variant of the above, I was once at a publishing event in France where my French translator of the current book introduced himself to me, bearing in train a copy of the book, a pistol, and a photographer. He wanted a photo of me, holding the book with an expression of outrage while I prepared to shoot him.

My opportunities to be an editor are rare, so I grab them when they come along. "No, no, not like that," I said, rewriting the poor man's concept. The photo we wound up with shows me staring in horror at an open copy of the book, with the gun to *my* head, while the translator is doubling toward the floor, helpless with mirth. (I had wanted him merely to stand there looking innocent, but he couldn't handle the assignment. You have to learn to live these parts.)

Later that same day, there was a formal luncheon, during which I became willy-nilly a party to one of the strangest formal-luncheon conversations of my life. The particular novel that had just been translated, in English *Two Much*, started: "It all began innocently enough; I wanted to get laid." The entire lunch conversation, gentlemen in suits and ties, ladies in frocks, concerned the one-and-only best French version of that sentence, or at least its conclusion. I don't speak

French, but apparently an amazing amount of obscenity ran around that table among the heavy silver and the cut glass goblets. One phrase was too crude, another too ambiguous. Everyone at the table agreed my translator had come up with absolutely the worst possibility, one that suggested the speaker merely wanted to go to sleep. So maybe his first idea, that I should shoot *him*, was best after all.

My oddest interaction with a translator, or at least with his work, came in Barcelona. Once the 700-year reign of Francisco Franco had ended, many things in Spain changed. Almodóvar sprang from the forehead of Venus, for instance. And the language grew. Under Franco, it was well known that no one spoke that ancient language Catalan, because he had banned it. Once everybody was positive the Generalissimo was really and truly and cross-your-heart dead, it turned out there were six million speakers of Catalan. Road signs in Catalan went up, shop window ads spoke in Catalan, and in Barcelona, the Center of Catalonia, there blossomed Catalan publishers. One of these, Ediciones 62, published my very first comic mystery, called in English, for reasons I've never understood, *The Fugitive Pigeon*. In launching this new venture, the publishers brought a

few writers to Barcelona to generate ink. At a press con-
ference, I was asked, "Why, in your book, do you say that
only Catalonians are awake in New York City at five
o'clock in the morning?"

What? I had no idea what he was talking about. A
copy of the book was produced, in Catalan, which
didn't help me much, but then another copy was found
in English, a language I could reasonably navigate, and
the passage was found. I had written "Authors who
come to New York from Mallorca once every ten years
to buy a new bathing suit always put down in their
books that the big city never sleeps, but that's what
they know. New York sleeps, all right, from about four-
thirty in the morning till about quarter after five." And
that's the point where my new friend dropped in his
observation about Catalonians.

What a wonderful moment! He could not have
dreamed, when he wrote that, that he'd be in communication with the first writer. It was accident piled on
happenstance to make it possible.

But communication did take place. In adding that
sentence, and then in that sentence finding its way to
me, he had told me, better than all the pictures of

translators with guns in their hands, just what kind of job this was.

Everything's a *joke* in this book! Everything is local references! Look at the hour, look how *long* it's taking me to turn this clumsy English into my beautiful Catalan! What does this American know of how I suffer?

Of all my collaborators, deliberate or accidental, that one is my favorite. He put his passion, his story, his humanity into my book without hurting my book. By adding one of *his* local jokes, he made the Catalonian edition richer, tastier than the original.

CONTRIBUTORS

Poet, writer, performer, teacher, actress, playwright, director, civil rights activist, and more, MAYA ANGELOU was born in St. Louis and grew up in Stamps, Arkansas. Her six-volume autobiography began with the publication of *I Know Why the Caged Bird Sings* in 1970, and concluded with *A Song Flung Up to Heaven*, published in the spring of 2003. Thirty-one honorary degrees are among the scores of prestigious awards and honors she has garnered from around the world. Dr. Angelou resides in Winston-Salem, North Carolina, where she is the first Reynolds Professor of American Studies at Wake Forest University, a lifetime appointment she has held since 1981.

LAWRENCE BLOCK's novels range from the urban *noir* of Matthew Scudder (*Hope to Die*) to the urbane effervescence of Bernie Rhodenbarr (*The Burglar in the Rye*), while other characters include the globe-trotting insomniac Evan Tanner (*Tanner on Ice*) and the introspective assassin Keller (*Hit List*). He has published articles and short fiction in *American Heritage, Redbook, Playboy, Cosmopolitan, GQ,* and *The New York Times,* and eighty-four of his short stories have been collected in *Enough Rope.* His newest bestseller is *Small Town,* a novel of post-9/11 New York. Larry is a Grand Master of Mystery Writers of America and a past president of both MWA and the Private Eye Writers of America. He has won the Edgar and Shamus awards four times each and the Japanese Maltese Falcon award twice, as well as the Nero Wolfe and Philip Marlowe awards, and, most recently, a Life Achievement Award from the Private Eye Writers of America. In France, he has been proclaimed a Grand Maitre du Roman Noir and has twice been awarded the Societe 813 trophy. He has been a guest of honor at Bouchercon and at book fairs and mystery festivals in France, Germany, Australia, Italy, New Zealand, and Spain, and, as if that were not enough, was presented with the key to the city of Munice, Indiana. Larry and his wife, Lynne, are enthusiastic New Yorkers and relentless world travelers.

A native New Yorker, TONYA BOLDEN graduated *magna cum laude* from Princeton University, with a degree in Slavic Languages and Literatures, and received her Master's degree in the same field from Columbia University. She has written, edited, or served as co-author of more than twenty books for adults and children, including *And Not Afraid To Dare: The Stories of Ten African American Women*, *33 Things Every Girl Should Know*, and *Tell All the Children Our Story: Memories & Mementos of Being Young and Black in America*, which was designated a 2002 School Library Journal Book of the Year.

MEG CABOT was born in Bloomington, Indiana. After receiving a B.A. degree from Indiana University, she moved to New York, where she quickly abandoned her original dream of becoming an illustrator, took a job as assistant manager of an undergraduate dormitory at New York University, and proceeded to write in her spare time. In addition to her romance novels (written as Patricia Cabot, and, more recently, Meggin Cabot),

she writes several series of books for young adult readers, including *The Princess Diaries*, *The Mediator*, and
1-800-WHERE-R-YOU, as well as the bestselling *All
American Girl*. Ms. Cabot lives in New York with her
husband and one-eyed cat, Henrietta.

CHARLOTTE CARTER grew up in Chicago and later
resided for periods of time in North Africa, France, and
Canada, but she has lived most of her life in New York.
She was a poet on the downtown Manhattan scene in the
1970s and 1980s, and also a freelance editor and ghost
writer. In the 1990s, she turned to crime-writing, produc-
ing three novels—*Rhode Island Red*, *Coq au Vin*, and
Drumsticks—in her critically acclaimed Nanette Hayes
series featuring a young, black musician who is also an
amateur sleuth. A change of pace followed with *Walking
Bones*, a novel about an explosive urban love affair. In
2003, Ms. Carter returned to detective fiction, and to her
roots, with *Jackson Park*, the inaugural volume in a new
Cook County series she sets in 1960s Chicago.

Born and raised in the Depression-era Bronx, an up-
bringing she describes affectionately in her memoir,

Kitchen Privileges, MARY HIGGINS CLARK achieved international fame as a writer against heavy odds. Left a young widow with five children to raise after her first husband died of a heart attack in 1964, she earned a living writing radio scripts, stealing the hours from five to seven A.M. for herself to try her hand at writing books. Her first suspense novel, *Where Are the Children?*, was published in 1975 and became a bestseller. That success freed her to pursue a college education; four years later, she graduated from Fordham University at Lincoln Center with a B.A. degree in philosophy, *summa cum laude*. Twenty-eight bestsellers later, she is a Mystery Writers of America Grand Master, and has been awarded a vast array of honors, including eighteen honorary doctorates. She lives in Saddle River, New Jersey.

Named United States Poet Laureate 2001–2003, BILLY COLLINS has long enchanted audiences on National Public Radio and at his readings in various venues across the country. His collections of poetry include *Sailing Alone Around the Room*, *Nine Horses*, *Questions About Angels*, *The Art of Drowning*, and *Picnic, Lightning*. He also selected the poems and wrote the introduction for the anthology *Poetry 180: A Turning Back to Poetry*. His work has appeared in *The New Yorker, The Paris Review,* and *The American Scholar,* and he has won a number of prestigious prizes from *Poetry* magazine. Mr. Collins is Distinguished Professor of English at Lehman College, City University of New York and a New York Public Library "Literary Lion." Among his other honors are fellowships from the New York Foundation for the Arts, the National Endowment for the Arts, and the Guggenheim Foundation. He lives in Somers, New York.

EDWIDGE DANTICAT was born in Haiti and moved to the United States when she was twelve. She is the author of several books, including *Breath, Eyes, Memory,* an Oprah's Book Club selection, *Krik? Krak!*, a National Book Award finalist, and *The Farming of Bones,* an American Book Award winner. She is also the editor of *The Butterfly's Way: Voices from the Haitian Dyaspora in the United States* and *The Beacon Best of 2000: Great Writing by Women of All Colors and Cultures.*

KENNETH C. DAVIS is the creator of the *Don't Know Much About*® series, beginning with *Don't Know Much About History.* That book spent thirty-five weeks on the *New York Times* bestseller list, and has since been joined by volumes on geography, the Civil War, the Bible, and the universe. The author subsequently launched two additional *Don't Know Much About* series, extending his concept of making learning fun to children. For young children, picture books cover such subjects as the fifty states, the solar system, the presidents, and the pilgrims; for middle graders, topics include planet Earth and American history. Mr. Davis has an honorary Doctor of Humane Letters from Concordia College. Born in the New York suburb of Mount Vernon, he now lives in Manhattan.

NELSON DEMILLE was born in New York City and grew up on Long Island, where he now lives. He left Hofstra University after three years to join the army, spending a year in Vietnam. He was decorated with the United States Army Air Medal, Bronze Star, and the Vietnamese Cross of Gallantry. At the end of his tour of duty, he returned to Hofstra, graduating with a degree in political science and history. He launched his writing career in 1973 with a series of police detective novels, and in 1978, his first major novel, *By the Rivers of Babylon*, was published and became a Book-of-the-Month-Club Main Selection. A stream of bestsellers followed, including *Word of Honor, The Gold Coast, Plum Island,* and *The General's Daughter,* which was made into a major motion picture starring John Travolta. In 2002, he published *Up Country,* which was inspired by a journey he took to revisit his old wartime battlegrounds. Mr. DeMille holds honorary doctorates from Hofstra University, Long Island University, and Dowling College and is a member of the Authors Guild, Mystery Writers of America, and MENSA.

PETE HAMILL is for many the quintessential New Yorker. Born in Brooklyn, he is the oldest of seven children of Irish immigrants from Belfast. At the age of sixteen, he left school to work in the Brooklyn Navy Yard, subsequently joining the Navy, where he completed his high school education. After studying painting and writing at Mexico City College, he worked for several years as a graphic designer in New York, while studying at Pratt Institute. In 1960, he joined the *New York Post* as a reporter, and a long and illustrious career in journalism ensued. He has served as Editor-in-Chief of both the *New York Post* and the New York *Daily News,* and has been a columnist for both those newspapers, as well as for New York *Newsday.* His articles have appeared in all the major magazines, including *Esquire, New York*, and *The New York Times* Magazine; he is currently on the staff of *The New Yorker*. His books include a memoir, *A Drinking Life*, and the novel *Snow in August*—both *New York Times* bestsellers. In 1999, Harry N. Abrams published his lavishly illustrated biography of the Mexican painter Diego Rivera. His magical new novel, *Forever*, spans 250 years of New York history, as seen through the eyes of a single larger-than-life character that has lived through it all. He divides his time between New York and Cuernavaca, Mexico.

OSCAR HIJUELOS was born to Cuban immigrants on New York's Upper West Side, a neighborhood that continues to inform his writing. He attended Bronx Community College and received his B.A. degree from the City College of New York, before completing his studies at City College's graduate program. His first novel, *Our House in The Lost World*, made an impressive debut, garnering a number of awards, including the American Academy of Arts and Letters' Rome Prize and a fellowship from the National Endowment for the Arts. His second book, *The Mambo Kings Play Songs of Love*, won the Pulitzer Prize for Fiction and went on to become an enormously popular national and international bestseller. He has published four other novels: *The Fourteen Sisters of Emilio Montez O'Brien, Mr. Ives' Christmas, Empress of the Splendid Season,* and *A Simple Habana Melody (from when the world was good).* Mr. Hijuelos enjoys traveling to many parts of the world, but still makes his home in New York, not far from the neighborhood in which he was raised.

Cultural critic, feminist theorist, and writer bell hooks was named one of *Utne Reader*'s "100 Visionaries Who Could Change Your Life." Born in Hopkinsville, Kentucky, she uses a pseudonym to honor both her grandmother (whose name she took) and her mother. A charismatic speaker, she divides her time among teaching, writing, and lecturing assignments around the world. She received her B.A. from Stanford University, M.A. from the University of Wisconsin, and Ph.D. from the University of California at Santa Cruz. Ms. hooks is the author of more than twenty books, including *Rock My Soul: Black People and Self-Esteem; Communion: The Female Search for Love; Salvation: Black People and Love; Remembered Rapture: The Writer at Work; Killing Rage: Ending Racism,* and with

Cornel West, *Breaking Bread: Insurgent Black Intellectual Life*. She has written children's books *Happy to Be Nappy* and *Be Boy Buzz*, illustrated by Christopher Raschka. She lives in New York City.

A native of Mansfield, Louisiana, WADE HUDSON began writing at a young age. The author of nearly twenty books for children, he has also been a newspaper reporter, public relations specialist, playwright, and songwriter. His passion for writing and lifelong mission to help foster positive self-image within the young black community helped propel the launch of Just Us Books, the children's book publishing company he and his wife, Cheryl, founded in 1998. Among his books are *AFRO-BETS Book of Black Heroes From A to Z*, *Jamal's Busy Day*, *I Love My Family*, *Pass It On: African-American Poetry for Children*, *Book of Black Heroes: Scientists, Healers and Inventors*, and *Five Brave Explorers*. With Cheryl Hudson, he has collaborated on a number of books, including *How Sweet the Sound: African-American Songs for Children*, *In Praise of Our Fathers and Our Mothers*, and *Kids Book of Wisdom: Quotes from the African-American Tradition*. He serves on the boards of many organizations, including the Children's Defense Fund's

Langston Hughes Library at the Alex Haley Farm, and is the recipient of the Stephen Crane Literary Award and other honors. The Hudsons live in New Jersey.

EVAN HUNTER's career has spanned almost five decades, from his first novel, *The Blackboard Jungle*, to his most recent, *The Moment She Was Gone*. The author of more than eighty mysteries and police procedurals, Mr. Hunter writes under several names, but most famously as either Evan Hunter or Ed McBain. The two even teamed up to write a book in tandem: *Candyland*. He has also written many screenplays, including Alfred Hitchcock's *The Birds*. As Ed McBain, he has created fifty-two 87th Precinct novels to date, the latest of which are *Money, Money, Money* and *Fat Ollie's Book*. Books by Evan Hunter/Ed McBain are bestsellers in more than two dozen countries. A Mystery Writers of America Grand Master for lifetime achievement, he was the first American to receive the British Crime Writers Association Cartier Diamond Dagger. He lives in Weston, Connecticut.

Novelist, essayist, and screenwriter SUSAN ISAACS was born in Brooklyn and educated at Queens College. She held the position of senior editor at *Seventeen* magazine, and later worked as a freelance writer of political speeches and magazine articles while her children were young. Her first novel, *Compromising Positions*, a whodunit set on suburban Long Island, was the first of a string of bestsellers, which include *Close Relations, Almost Paradise,* and *Shining Through.* The sequel to her first novel, *Long Time No See,* is her most recent bestseller. In addition to her popular fiction, she is the author of the book *Dames and Wimpettes: What Women Are Really Doing on Page and Screen* and a series of columns on the 2000 presidential campaign, published by *Newsday.* Currently chairman of the board of Poets & Writers, and a past president of Mystery Writers of America, she is a member of numerous writers' groups and has been active in several anti-censorship campaigns. She also sits on the boards of the Queens College Foundation, the Nassau County Coalition Against Domestic Violence, and other community organizations. She lives on Long Island.

A longtime city and sports columnist for *The New York Times,* ROBERT LIPSYTE is the author of sixteen books, including *In the Country of Illness: Comfort and Advice for the Journey, Sports World: An American*

Dreamland, and the young adult novels *The Contender*, *One Fat Summer*, and *Warrior Angel*. He is a former network correspondent for CBS and NBC, and won an Emmy for on-camera work as host of the nightly WNET public affairs broadcast, *The Eleventh Hour*. He also hosted *The Health Show*, a weekly live half-hour of medical and health-related reportage on Cablevision. He has twice won Columbia University's Meyer Berger Award for distinguished reporting. His ability to write for young people was recognized by the American Li-brary Association, which bestowed upon him its Mar-garet A. Edwards award for lifetime achievement in young adult literature. He lives in Manhattan.

FRANK MCCOURT was born in New York and raised in Limerick, Ireland. At the age of nineteen, he returned to the United States to seek his fortune. He graduated from New York University's School of Education and supported himself with several odd jobs before he found his first calling, and commenced a long career as a New York City public high school teacher—the last seventeen years of which were spent at the prestigious Stuyvesant High School. In 1996, after he retired from teaching, his memoir about his childhood, *Angela's Ashes,* was published, and held the top position on bestseller lists across the country for many months. The book won the Pulitzer Prize and many other awards, and was selected as the #1 nonfiction book of the year by both *Time* and *Newsweek* magazines. When his follow-up volume, *'Tis: A Memoir*, was published, it occupied the top spot on *The New York Times* bestseller list at the same time the earlier book was in first place on the paperback list. The author's storytelling skills are often on display in theatrical settings. His musical revue, *The Irish and How They Got That Way*, ran for more than a year at the Irish Repertory Theatre in New York. Much in demand as a lecturer, he is the recipient of numerous honorary degrees. He lives in Connecticut, where he is working on his third book, a memoir about teaching.

GITA MEHTA is the author of two novels, *Raj* and *The River Sutra*, and two nonfiction works, *Karma Cola: Marketing the Mystic East* and *Snakes and Ladders: Glimpses of Modern India*. She has written, produced, and directed a number of documentaries for American, British, and European television, and also contributed articles to Indian, European, and American publications. Educated in India and at Cambridge

University, she divides her time between New York, London, and India.

Born and raised in St. Louis, Missouri, DANNY MEYER is now New York's premier restaurateur. He grew up loving to cook, and after graduating from Trinity College with a political science degree, he eventually made his way to New York, where he pursued his passions for food and wine. He became an assistant manager at the seafood restaurant Pesca and then studied cooking in Italy and France. In 1985, at the age of twenty-seven, he launched his first restaurant, Union Square Cafe; nine years later, with chef/partner Tom Colicchio, he opened Gramercy Tavern. The two establishments have consistently earned the top two rankings on the Zagat Survey's list of New York's Most Popular Restaurants. Eleven Madison Park and Tabla were introduced a few years later, each making Zagat's Top 20 list in their early years. Blue Smoke and the jazz club Jazz Standard followed in 2002. He is the co-author, with Michael Romano, of *Union Square Cafe Cookbook* and *Second Helpings from Union Square Cafe*. An active leader in the fight against hunger, Mr. Meyer serves on the boards of Share Our Strength and City Harvest. He and his restaurants have

won an unprecedented ten James Beard Awards and numerous other culinary and community honors. He lives
in New York.

MARY POPE OSBORNE grew up in the military. By
the time she was fifteen, she had lived in seven different
places. After graduating from the University of North
Carolina at Chapel Hill, she had many adventures, camp-
ing in a cave in Crete, and later traveling through sixteen
Asian countries with a small band of young people. Her
first young adult book was *Run, Run As Fast As You Can*.
Now, over twenty years and fifty books later, she has contributed widely to the field of children's and young adult
literature, penning novels, picture books, biographies,
mysteries, and retellings of fairy tales, myths and tall
tales. Best known for her *Magic Tree House* series for
ages 5 to 8, she treasures the countless stories children
write in the same mode and share with her. With her
husband, Will Osborne, she has also created a nonfiction
companion series *Magic Tree House Research Guides*.
Her *New York's Bravest*, the story of a Paul Bunyan-like
legendary firefighter who actually lived in New York
in the 1840s, was published in 2002 and dedicated to
the New York City firemen who lost their lives on

September 11, 2001. Ms. Osborne served four years as president of the Authors Guild, and is currently a member of the Board of Directors. She lives in New York.

CYNTHIA OZICK is the author of novels, short stories, essays, and a play. Her most recent collection of essays, *Quarrel & Quandary*, won a National Critics Circle Award for Non-Fiction as well as a Koret Foundation Prize for Literary Studies. Among numerous other honors, she has received a PEN/Spiegel-Diamondstein Award for the Art of the Essay and a Lannan Foundation Award for Fiction. She is a member of the Academy of Arts and Letters.

WILLIE PERDOMO is the author of *Where a Nickel Costs a Dime*. His work has been included in several anthologies, among them *The Harlem Reader, Poems of New York,* and *Bum Rush the Page: A Def Poetry Jam.* His work has also appeared in *The New York Times* magazine, Russell Simmons' *One World* magazine, and *Pen America: A Journal for Writers and Readers.* He is the author of *Visiting Langston,* a Coretta Scott King Honor Book for Children, illustrated by Bryan Collier. He has also been featured on the PBS documentary

"The United States of Poetry," and HBO's "Def Poetry Jam." His fiction has been published in the anthologies *Wachale!: Growing up Latino in the USA* and *Brown Sugar 2: A Collection of Erotic Black Fiction*. Mr. Perdomo has taught workshops for the Cave Canem Foundation, Bronx Writer's Center, and Friends Seminary. His new collection, *Smoking Lovely*, will be published in Fall 2003 by Rattapallax Press.

ROBERT PINSKY was born in Long Branch, New Jersey. He studied at Rutgers University and Stanford University, where he held a Stegner Fellowship. His books of poetry include *Jersey Rain*, *The Figured Wheel*, and *An Explanation of America*. His most recent book of prose is *Democracy, Culture and the Voice of Poetry*. His landmark translation *The Inferno of Dante* was awarded the Landon Translation Prize and the *Los Angeles Times* Book Award. He is a contributor to *The NewsHour with Jim Lehrer* and his essays, poems, and reviews appear regularly in *The Atlantic Monthly*, *The New Yorker*, *The New Republic*, *The Paris Review*, and other magazines. He has won numerous poetry prizes, among them the William Carlos Williams Prize, the

Shelley Memorial Award, and the Lenore Marshall Prize. His other honors and awards include honorary degrees from Rutgers, the University of Michigan, Northwestern University, and Stanford University. He has served as Poetry Editor of *Slate* since 1996. Professor of English and Creative Writing at Boston University since 1988, he taught previously at the University of California, Berkeley. As Poet Laureate of the United States from 1997 to 2000, he founded the Favorite Poem Project.

Celebrated poet MARIE PONSOT is a native New Yorker. Her published works include *Springing,* which won the Phi Beta Kappa Prize, and *The Bird Catcher,* winner of the National Book Critics Circle Award. Her other books include *The Green Dark*, *Admit Impediment*, and *True Minds*. Ms. Ponsot, who also translates books in French, has taught in the graduate programs at Queens College, Beijing United University, the Poetry Center of the YMHA, and New York University. Among her awards are a creative writing grant from the National Endowment for the Arts, the Delmore Schwartz Memorial Prize, and the Shaughnessy

Medal of the Modern Language Association. She lives in New York, where she teaches at various writing programs.

RUTH REICHL, editor-in-chief of *Gourmet* magazine, grew up in New York's Greenwich Village, the scene of many memorable meals. By the 1970s, she had roamed far from home and was the chef and co-owner of The Swallow Restaurant in Berkeley, California. Her first book, *Mmmmm: A Feastiary*, was published during that decade. Along the way, she acquired her B.A. and M.A. degrees in History of Art from the University of Michigan. She is the author of two bestselling memoirs, *Tender at the Bone* and *Comfort Me With Apples*, and she is also the editor of The Modern Library Cooking series and *Endless Feasts: Sixty Years of Writing from Gourmet*. She is currently editing *The Gourmet Cookbook* to be released in 2004. She has earned three James Beard Awards (one for restaurant criticism; two for journalism). For the Food Network, Reichl hosted three one-hour television specials covering New York, San Francisco, and Miami. She served as restaurant critic for *New West* and *California* magazines, the *Los*

Angeles Times, and *The New York Times,* before joining *Gourmet* magazine as editor-in-chief in 1999. She
lives in New York, where she is active in food-related
and environmental organizations.

Born in San Juan, Puerto Rico, ESMERALDA SAN-
TIAGO arrived in New York at the age of thirteen, the
eldest in a family of eleven children. She majored in
drama and dance at the High School of Performing
Arts, studied part-time at community colleges, and
subsequently transferred to Harvard University on a
full scholarship, graduating *magna cum laude.* With
her husband, Frank Cantor, she founded a film production company, and her writing career evolved from her
work in documentary and educational films. She is the
author of two memoirs, *When I Was Puerto Rican* and
Almost A Woman. The latter was adapted for television's Masterpiece Theatre, winning the George Foster
Peabody Award. Ms. Santiago has also published a
novel, *América's Dream,* and co-edited with Joie Davi-
dow two anthologies, *Las Christmas: Favorite Latino
Authors Share Their Holiday Memories,* and *Las
Mamis: Favorite Latino Authors Remember Their*

Mothers. Her essays and opinion pieces have appeared in newspapers and magazines, and as guest commentary on National Public Radio. She serves on the boards of arts and literature organizations, and has designed community-based programs for adolescents and battered women and their children. Her awards and honors include a Girl Scouts of America National Woman of Distinction Award, and honorary doctorates from Trinity University and Pace University. She lives in Westchester County, New York.

Former firefighter DENNIS SMITH worked for eighteen years in some of the City's most difficult and dangerous districts. *Report From Engine Co. 82,* his 1972 account of life in the South Bronx firehouse in which he served, became an immediate bestseller and is now an authentic classic. The author, who holds a B.A. degree in English and an M.A. in Communications from New York University, went on to write ten more books, and also founded *Firehouse* magazine. His published works include *Glitter and Ash, The Final Fire, Firehouse, Firefighters—Their Lives in Their Own Words,* and other works of fiction and nonfiction. His most recent book is *Report from Ground Zero,* a historical account of September 11, 2001, as seen from the front lines. Dennis Smith's career began in the New York Fire Department and his heart has never strayed far from it. From his book royalties, he created the Foundation for American Firefighters to support health and safety efforts and burn care facilities. He became a licensed financial advisor, and created Affinity Financial Services for Firefighters, working with banks to offer credit card and mortgage programs. His dedication and service have been recognized in awards from the Congressional Fire Services Institute, the National Fire Academy, the International Association of Fire Chiefs, and more. His community service extends beyond the fire department. He has headed the Kips Bay Boys and Girls Club in the Bronx for almost twenty years, serves on the national board of advisors of Boys and Girls Clubs of America, and is a past chairman of the New York Academy of Art. He lives in New York.

R. L. STINE was born and grew up in Columbus, Ohio, where he began to write at the age of nine. Shortly after graduating from Ohio State University, he moved to New York, where he lives today. In the early 1990s, his *Goosebumps* series made its debut. In 2000 and

2001, the books had broken all records, and R. L. Stine took his place in the Guinness Book of Records as the world's #1 bestselling author of a children's book series—with more than 215 million copies sold. His wicked imagination has also produced *The Nightmare Room* and *Fear Street* series. His anthology, *Beware! R.L. Stine Picks His Favorite Scary Stories,* won the Disney Adventures Kids' Choice Award for Best Mystery/Horror book, an honor also given to his *Nightmare Hour* and *The Nightmare Room #2* in previous years. He has also received several Nickelodeon Kids' Choice Awards, among his numerous honors. He is involved in a number of film, video, and DVD projects, including *When Good Ghouls Go Bad,* a direct-to-TV film he produced for Fox Family Channel, and *R. L. Stine's Haunted Lighthouse,* a spooky, but family-friendly adventure film. His newest book is *Dangerous Girls.*

PETER STRAUB was born in Milwaukee. Mr. Straub graduated from the University of Wisconsin with honors in English and obtained his Master's degree from Columbia University. Returning to his home state to teach English at his high school alma mater, he developed a passion for poetry. Not long after, he traveled to Dublin to work on a Ph.D., and wound up publishing two small books of poems and a first novel, *Marriages*. Moving to London for a time, he wrote *Ghost Story*, the first of sixteen novels and works of short fiction, many of them bestsellers—including *Koko and Mr. X*—and two collaborations with Stephen King, *The Talisman* and *Black House*. His latest spinetingler, *lost boy lost girl*, is scheduled for publication in Fall 2003. Mr. Straub is a member of Horror Writers of America, Mystery Writers of America, PEN, and the Adams Round Table. He lives on Manhattan's Upper West Side.

The creator of John Dortmunder, DONALD E. WESTLAKE was born in Brooklyn, grew up in Albany, attended the State University of New York, and served in the United States Air Force. Under his own name, or as "Richard Stark" or "Tucker Coe," he has entertained a vast international audience with over seventy mystery novels. Stark's early book, *The Hunter*, was the basis for the film noir classic, *Point Blank*, as well as the 1998 remake, *Payback*. Among Westlake's most popular creations are *The Ax*, *Trust Me On This*, and ten novels featuring the ex-con John Dortmunder and his hapless accomplices. They include *The Hot Rock*, which became a film classic, *Bank Shot*, and *Bad News*. Westlake was nominated for an Academy Award for his screenplay of *The Grifters;* his screenwriting credits also include *Cops and Robbers* and *The Stepfather*. His first book, *The Mercenaries*, was nominated for the MWA Edgar Award as the best first novel of the year. Mr. Westlake is a Mystery Writers of America Grand Master, and has been honored with three Edgars, a Lifetime Achievement Award at the Bouchercon convention, and the Writers Guild of America's Ian McLellan Hunter Award for Lifetime Achievement. He also holds an honorary doctorate from SUNY Binghamton. His latest book is *Money for Nothing*. Messrs. Westlake, Stark and Coe live in upstate New York.